Principles of Orchestration

By

Nikolay Rimsky-Korsakov

Edited by
MAXIMILIAN STEINBERG

English translation by
EDWARD AGATE

VOLUME I

ISBN-13:
978-1537633541

ISBN-10:
1537633546

Note: This is an historical text. Original page numbers can be found in brackets throughout this publication

Editor's Preface.

Rimsky-Korsakov had long been engrossed in his treatise on orchestration. We have in our possession a thick note book of some 200 pages in fine hand writing, dating from the years 1873-1874, containing a monograph on the question of acoustics, a classification of wind instruments and a detailed description of the construction and fingering of the different kinds of flute, the oboe, clarinet and horn.[1]

In his "Memoirs of my musical life" (1st edition, p. 120) the following passage occurs: "I had planned to devote all my energies to the compilation of a full treatise on orchestration. To this end I made several rough copies, jotting down explanatory notes detailing the technique of different instruments. What I intended to present to the world on this subject, was to include *everything*. The writing of this treatise, or, to be more exact, the sketch for it took up most of my time in the years 1873 and 1874. After reading the works of Tyndall and Helmholtz, I framed an introduction to my work, in which I endeavoured to expound the laws of acoustics as applied to the principles governing the construction of musical instruments. My manual was to begin with a detailed list of instruments, classified in groups and tabulated, including a description of the various systems in use at the present day. I had not yet thought of the second part of the book which was to be devoted to instruments in combination. But I soon realised that I had gone too far. With wind instruments in particular, the different systems were innumerable, and each manufacturer favoured his own pet theory. By the addition of a certain key the maker endowed his instrument with the possibility of a new trill, and- VIII- made some difficult passages more playable than on an instrument of another kind.

"There was no end to such complications. In the brass, I found instruments with three, four, and five valves, the mechanism varying according to the make. Obviously, I could not hope to cover so large a field; besides, of what value would such a treatise be to the student? Such a mass of detailed description of the various systems, their advantages and drawbacks, could not but fail to confuse the reader only too eager to learn. Naturally he would wish to know what instrument to employ, the extent of its capabilities etc., and getting no satisfactory information he would throw my massive work aside. For these reasons my interest in the book gradually waned, and finally I gave up the task."

In 1891 Rimsky-Korsakov, now an artist of standing, the composer of *Snegourotchka*, *Mlada*, and *Shéhérazade*, a master of the orchestral technique he had been teaching for twenty years, returned to his handbook on instrumentation. He would seem to have made notes at different times from 1891 to 1893, during which period, after the first performance of *Mlada*, he gave up composition for a while. These notes, occasionally referred to in his *Memoirs*, are in three volumes of manuscript-paper. They contain the unfinished preface of 1891, a paragraph full of clear, thoughtful writing, and reprinted in this book.[2]

As the author tells us in his *Memoirs* (p. 297), the progress of his work was hampered by certain troublesome events which were happening at the time. Dissatisfied with his rough draft, he destroyed the greater part of it, and once more abandoned his task.

In 1894 he composed *The Christmas Night*; this was the beginning of his most fertile period. He became entirely engrossed in composition, making plans for a fresh opera as soon as the one in hand was completed. It was not until 1905 that his thoughts returned to the treatise on orchestration, his musical output remaining in abeyance through no fault of his own. Since 1891 the plan of the work had been entirely remodelled, as proved by the rough drafts still extant. The author had given up the idea of describing different instruments from their technical -IX- standpoint, and was more anxious to dwell upon the value of tone qualities and their various combinations.

Among the author's papers several forms of the book have been found, each widely differing in detail from the other. At last, in the summer of 1905 Rimsky-Korsakov brought his plans to a head, and outlined the six chapters which form the foundation of the present volume. But the work suffered a further interruption, and the sketches were once more laid aside. In his *Memoirs*, Rimsky-Korsakov explains the fact by lack of interest in the work and a general feeling of weariness: "The treatise remained in abeyance. To start with, the form of the book was not a success, and I awaited the production of *Kitesh*, in order to give some examples from that work" (p. 360).

Then came the autumn of 1906. The composer experienced another rush of creative energy; his opera, *The Golden Cockerel* made rapid strides, and kept him busy all that winter and the following summer. When it was finished, in the autumn of 1907, his thoughts reverted to the treatise on orchestration. But the work made little progress. The author had his doubts as to the adequacy of the plan he had adopted, and, in spite of the entreaties of his pupils and friends, he could not bring himself to broach the latter part of the book. Towards the end of 1907 Rimsky-Korsakov was constantly ailing in health, and this materially affected his energy. He spent the greater part of his time reading old notes and classifying examples. About the 20th of May he set out for his summer residence in Lioubensk, and having just recovered from a third severe attack of inflammation of the lungs, began to work on the first chapter of the treatise in its present, final form. This chapter was finished on June 7/20, about 4 o'clock in the afternoon; the same night, the composer was seized with a fourth attack which proved fatal.

The honour fell on me to prepare this last work of Rimsky-Korsakov for publication. Now that *Principles of Orchestration* has appeared in print I think it necessary to devote a few words to the essential features of the book, and to the labour imposed upon me in my capacity as editor.

On the first point I will say but little. The reader will observe from the Contents that the work differs from others, not merely by -X- reason of its musical examples, but more especially in the systematic arrangement of material, not according to orchestral division in groups (the method adopted by Gevaert for instance), but according to *each constituent of the musical whole, considered separately*. The orchestration of melodic and harmonic elements (Chapters II and III) receives special attention, as does the question of orchestration in general (Chapter IV). The last two chapters are devoted to operatic music, and the sixth takes a supplementary form, having no direct bearing on the previous matter.

Rimsky-Korsakov altered the title of his book several times, and his final choice was never made. The title I have selected seems to me to be the one most suitable to the contents of the work, "principles" in the truest sense of the word. Some may expect to find the "secrets" of the great orchestrator disclosed; but, as he himself reminds us in his preface, "to orchestrate is to create, and this is something which cannot be taught."

Yet, as invention, in all art, is closely allied to technique, this book may reveal much to the student of instrumentation. Rimsky-Korsakov has often repeated the axiom that *good orchestration means proper handling of parts*. The simple use of tone-colours and their combinations may also be taught, but there the science of instruction ends. From these standpoints the present book will furnish the pupil with nearly everything he requires. The author's death prevented him from discussing a few questions, amongst which I would include full polyphonic orchestration and the scoring of melodic and harmonic designs. But these questions can be partly solved by the principles laid down in Chapters II and III, and I have no wish to overcrowd the first edition of this book with extra matter which can be added later, if it is found to be necessary. I had first of all to prepare and amplify the sketches made by Rimsky-Korsakov in 1905; these form a connected summary throughout the whole six chapters. Chapter I was completed by the author; it is published as it stands, save for a few unimportant alterations in style. As regards the other five chapters, I have tried to keep to the original drafts as far as possible, and have only made a few changes in the order, and one or two indispensable additions. The sketches made between 1891 and 1893 were too disconnected to be of much use, but, in point -XI- of fact, they corresponded very closely to the final form of the work.

The musical examples are of greater importance. According to the original scheme, as noted on the 1891 MS., they were to be drawn from the works of Glinka and Tschaikovsky; those of Borodin and Glazounov were to be added later. The idea of choosing examples solely from his own works only came to Rimsky-Korsakov by degrees. The reasons for this decision are partly explained in the unfinished preface of 1905, but other motives may be mentioned. If Rimsky-Korsakov had chosen his examples from the works of these four composers, he would have had to give some account of their individual, and often strongly marked peculiarities of style. This would have been a difficult undertaking, and then, how to justify the exclusion of West-European composers, Richard Wagner, for example, whose orchestration Rimsky-Korsakov so greatly admired? Besides, the latter could hardly fail to realise that his own compositions afforded sufficient material to illustrate every conceivable manner of scoring, examples *emanating from one great general principle*. This is not the place to criticise his method; Rimsky-Korsakov's "school" is here displayed, each may examine it for himself. The brilliant, highly-coloured orchestration of Russian composers, and the scoring of the younger French musicians are largely developments of the methods of Rimsky-Korsakov, who, in turn, looked upon Glinka as his spiritual father.

The table of examples found among the author's papers was far from complete; some portions were badly explained, others, not at all. The composer had not mentioned which musical quotations were to be printed in the second volume, and which examples were to indicate the study of the full score; further, no limit was fixed to the length of quotation. All this was therefore left to the editor's discretion. I selected the examples only after much doubt and hesitation, finding it difficult to keep to those stipulated by the composer, as every page of the master's works abounds in appropriate instances of this or that method of scoring.

I was guided by the following considerations which agreed with the opinions of the author himself: in the first place the examples should be as simple as possible, so as not to distract-XII- the student's attention from the point under discussion; secondly, it was necessary that one example should serve to illustrate several sections of the book, and lastly, the majority of quotations should be those mentioned by the author. These amount to 214, in the second volume; the remaining 98 were added by me. They are drawn, as far as possible, from Rimsky-Korsakov's dramatic music, since operatic full-scores are less accessible than those of symphonic works.[3]

At the end of Vol. II I have added three tables showing different ways of scoring full chords; all my additions to the text are marked with asterisks. I consider that the careful study of the examples contained in the second volume will be of the greatest use to the student *without replacing* the need for the study of other composers' scores. Broadly speaking, the present work should be studied together with the reading of full scores in general.

A few words remain to be said regarding Rimsky-Korsakov's intention to point out the faulty passages in his orchestral works, an intention expressed in his preface to the last edition. The composer often referred to the instructional value of such examinations. His purpose however was never achieved. It is not for me to select these examples, and I shall only mention two which were pointed out by the composer himself: 1. *The Legend of Tsar Saltan* 220, 7th bar—the theme in the brass is not sufficiently prominent the trombones being *tacet* (a mistake easily rectified); 2. *The Golden Cockerel* 233, bars 10-14, if the marks of expression are observed in the brass, the counter-melody on the violas and violoncellos doubled by the wood-wind will hardly be heard. Example 75 may also be mentioned, to which the note on page 63, in the text, refers. I will confine myself to these examples.

In conclusion I desire to express my deep gratitude to Madame Rimsky-Korsakov for having entrusted me with the task of editing this work, thereby providing me with the opportunity of performing a duty sacred to the memory of a master, held so deeply in reverence.

St. Petersburgh, December 1912.

MAXIMILIAN STEINBERG.

Extract from the Author's Preface (1891).

Our epoch, the post-Wagnerian age, is the age of brilliance and imaginative quality in orchestral tone colouring. Berlioz, Glinka, Liszt, Wagner, modern French composers—Delibes, Bizet and others; those of the new Russian school—Borodin, Balakirev, Glazounov and Tschaikovsky—have brought this side of musical art to its zenith; they have eclipsed, as colourists, their predecessors, Weber, Meyerbeer and Mendelssohn, to whose genius, nevertheless, they are indebted for their own progress. In writing this book my chief aim has been to provide the well-informed reader with the fundamental principles of modern orchestration from the standpoint of brilliance and imagination, and I have devoted considerable space to the study of tonal resonance and orchestral combination.

I have tried to show the student how to obtain a certain quality of tone, how to acquire uniformity of structure and requisite power. I have specified the character of certain melodic figures and designs peculiar to each instrument or orchestral group, and reduced these questions briefly and clearly to general principles; in short I have endeavoured to furnish the pupil with matter and material as carefully and minutely studied as possible. Nevertheless I do not claim to instruct him as to how such information should be put to artistic use, nor to establish my examples in their rightful place in the poetic language of music. For, just as a handbook of harmony, counterpoint, or form presents the student with harmonic or polyphonic matter, principles of construction, formal arrangement, and sound technical methods, but will never endow him with the talent for composition, so a treatise on orchestration can demonstrate how to produce a well-sounding chord-2- of certain tone-quality, uniformly distributed, how to detach a melody from its harmonic setting, correct progression of parts, and solve all such problems, but will never be able to teach the art of poetic orchestration. To orchestrate is to create, and this is something which cannot be taught.

It is a great mistake to say: this composer scores well, or, that composition is well orchestrated, for orchestration is *part of the very soul of the work*. A work is thought out in terms of the orchestra, certain tone-colours being inseparable from it in the mind of its creator and native to it from the hour of its birth. Could the essence of Wagner's music be divorced from its orchestration? One might as well say that a picture is well *drawn* in colours.

More than one classical and modern composer has lacked the capacity to orchestrate with imagination and power; the secret of colour has remained outside the range of his creative faculty. Does it follow that these composers do not *know how* to orchestrate? Many among them have had greater knowledge of the subject than the mere colourist. Was Brahms ignorant of orchestration? And yet, nowhere in his works do we find evidence of brilliant tone or picturesque fancy. The truth is that his thoughts did not turn towards colour; his mind did not exact it.

The power of subtle orchestration is a secret impossible to transmit, and the composer who possesses this secret should value it highly, and never debase it to the level of a mere collection of formulæ learned by heart.

Here I may mention the case of works scored by others from the composer's rough directions. He who undertakes such work should enter as deeply as he may into the spirit of the composer, try to realise his intentions, and develop them in all their essential features.

Though one's own personality be subordinate to that of another, such orchestration is nevertheless creative work. But on the other hand, to score a composition never intended for the orchestra, is an undesirable practice. Many musicians have made this mistake and persist in it.[4] In any case this is the lowest form of in-3-strumentation, akin to colour photography, though of course the process may be well or badly done.

As regards orchestration it has been my good fortune to belong to a first-rate school, and I have acquired the most varied experience. In the first place I have had the opportunity of hearing all my works performed by the excellent orchestra of the St. Petersburgh Opera. Secondly, having experienced leanings towards different directions, I have scored for orchestras of different sizes, beginning with simple combinations (my opera *The May Night* is written for natural horns and trumpets), and ending with the most advanced. In the third place, I conducted the choir of the Military Marine for several years and was therefore able to study wind-instruments. Finally I formed an orchestra of very young pupils, and succeeded in teaching them to play, quite competently, the works of Beethoven, Mendelssohn, Glinka, etc. All this has enabled me to present this work to the public as the result of long experience.

As a starting-point I lay down the following fundamental axioms:

I. *In the orchestra there is no such thing as ugly quality of tone.*

II. *Orchestral writing should be easy to play*; a composer's work stands the best chance when the parts are well written.[5]

III. *A work should be written for the size of orchestra that is to perform it*, not for some imaginary body, as many composers persist in doing, introducing brass instruments in unusual keys upon which the music is impracticable because it is not played in the key the composer intends.

It is difficult to devise any method of learning orchestration without a master. As a general rule it is best to advance by degrees from the simplest scoring to the most complicated.

The student will probably pass through the following phases: 1. the phase during which he puts his entire faith in percussion instru-4-ments, believing that beauty of sound emanates entirely from this branch of the orchestra—this is the earliest stage; 2. the period when he acquires a passion for the harp, using it in every possible chord; 3. the stage during which he adores the wood-wind and horns, using stopped notes in conjunction with strings, muted or *pizzicato*; 4. the more advanced period, when he has come to recognise that the string group is the richest and most expressive of all. When the student works alone he must try to avoid the pitfalls of the first three phases. The best plan is to study full-scores, and listen to an orchestra, score in hand. But it is difficult to decide what music should be studied and heard. Music of all ages, certainly, but, principally, that which is fairly modern. Fairly modern music will teach the student how to score—classical music will prove of negative value to him. Weber, Mendelssohn, Meyerbeer (*The Prophet*), Berlioz, Glinka, Wagner, Liszt, and modern French and Russian composers—these will prove his best guides. It is useless for a Berlioz or a Gevaert to quote examples from the works of Gluck. The musical idiom is too old-fashioned and strange to modern ears; such examples are of no further use today. The same may be said of Mozart and of Haydn (the father of modern orchestration).

The gigantic figure of Beethoven stands apart. His music abounds in countless leonine leaps of orchestral imagination, but his technique, viewed in detail, remains much inferior to his titanic conception. His use of the trumpets, standing out above the rest of the orchestra, the difficult and unhappy intervals he gives to the horns, the distinctive features of the string parts and his often highly-coloured employment of the wood-wind,—these features will combine causing the student of Beethoven to stumble upon a thousand and one points in contradiction.

It is a mistake to think that the beginner will light upon no simple and instructive examples in modern music, in that of Wagner and others. On the contrary, clearer, and better examples are to be found amongst modern composers than in what is called the range of classical music.

Extract from the Preface to the last edition.

My aim in undertaking this work is to reveal the principles of modern orchestration in a somewhat different light than that usually brought to bear upon the subject. I have followed these principles in orchestrating my own works, and, wishing to impart some of my ideas to young composers, I have quoted examples from my own compositions, or given references to them, endeavouring to show, in all sincerity, what is successful and what is not. No one can know except the author himself the purpose and motives which governed him during the composition of a certain work, and the practice of explaining the intentions of a composer, so prevalent amongst annotators, however reverent and discreet, appears to me far from satisfactory. They will attribute a too closely philosophic, or excessively poetic meaning to a plain and simple fact. Sometimes the respect which great composers' names command will cause inferior examples to be quoted as good; cases of carelessness or ignorance, easily explained by the imperfections of current technique, give rise to whole pages of laborious exposition, in defence, or even in admiration of a faulty passage.

This book is written for those who have already studied instrumentation from Gevaert's excellent treatise, or any other well-known manual, and who have some knowledge of a number of orchestral scores.

I shall therefore only just touch on such technical questions as fingering, range, emission of sound etc.[6]

The present work deals with the combination of instruments in separate groups and in the entire orchestral scheme; the different means of producing strength of tone and unity of structure; the sub-division of parts; variety of colour and expression in scoring,—the whole, principally from the standpoint of dramatic music.

Chapter I.

GENERAL REVIEW OF ORCHESTRAL GROUPS.

A. Stringed Instruments.

The following is the formation of the string quartet and the number of players required in present day orchestras, either in the theatre or concert-room.

	Full orchestra	Medium orchestra	Small orchestra
Violins I	16	12	8
" II	14	10	6
Violas	12	8	4
Violoncellos	10	6	3
Double basses	8-10	4-6	2-3

In larger orchestras, the number of first violins may amount to 20 and even 24, the other strings being increased proportionately. But such a great quantity of strings overpowers the customary wood-wind section, and entails re-inforcing the latter. Sometimes orchestras contain less than 8 first violins; this is a mistake, as the balance between strings and wind is completely destroyed. In writing for the orchestra it is advisable to rely on a medium-sized body of strings. Played by a larger orchestra a work will be heard to greater advantage; played by a smaller one, the harm done will be minimised.-7-

Whenever a group of strings is written for more than five parts—without taking double notes or chords into consideration—these parts may be increased by dividing each one into two, three and four sections, or even more (*divisi*). Generally, one or more of the principal parts is split up, the first or second violins, violas or violoncellos. The players are then divided by desks, numbers 1, 3, 5 etc. playing the upper part, and 2, 4, 6 etc., the lower; or else the musician on the right-hand of each desk plays the top line, the one on the left the bottom line. Dividing by threes is less easy, as the number of players in one group is not always divisible by three, and hence the difficulty of obtaining proper balance. Nevertheless there are cases where the composer should not hesitate to employ this method of dividing the strings, leaving it to the conductor to ensure equality of tone. It is always as well to mark how the passage is to be divided in the score; Vns I, 1, 2, 3 desks, 6 'Cellos div. à 3, and so on. Division into four and more parts is rare, but may be used in *piano* passages, as it greatly reduces volume of tone in the group of strings.

Note. In small orchestras passages sub-divided into many parts are very hard to realise, and the effect obtained is never the one required.

String parts may be divided thus:

$a \begin{cases} \text{Vns I div.} \\ \text{Vns II div.} \end{cases}$
$b \begin{cases} \text{Vns II div.} \\ \text{Violas div.} \end{cases}$
$c \begin{cases} \text{Violas div.} \\ \text{'Cellos div.} \end{cases}$
$d \begin{cases} \text{'Cellos div.} \\ \text{D. basses div.} \end{cases}$

Possible combinations less frequently used are:

$e \begin{cases} \text{Vns I div.} \\ \text{Violas div.} \end{cases}$
$f \begin{cases} \text{Vns II div.} \\ \text{'Cellos div.} \end{cases}$
$g \begin{cases} \text{Violas div.} \\ \text{D. basses div. etc.} \end{cases}$

Note. It is evident that the tone quality in *b* and *e* will be similar. Still *b* is preferable since the number of Vns II (14-10-6) and Violas (12-8-4) is practically the same, the respective rôles of the two groups are more closely allied, and from the fact that second violins generally sit nearer to the violas than the first, thereby guaranteeing greater unity in power and execution.

The reader will find all manner of divisions in the musical examples given in Vol. II. Where necessary, some explanation as to the method of dividing strings will follow in due course. I dwell on the subject here in order to show how the usual composition of the string quartet may be altered.-8-

Stringed instruments possess more ways of producing sound than any other orchestral group. They can pass, better than other instruments from one shade of expression to another, the varieties being of an infinite number. Species of bowing such as *legato*, detached, *staccato*, *spiccato*, *portamento*, *martellato*, light *staccato*, *saltando*, attack at the nut and at the point, ⊓ ⊓ ⊓ and V V V (down bow and up bow), in every degree of tone, *fortissimo*, *pianissimo*, *crescendo*, *diminuendo*, *sforzando*, *morendo*—all this belongs to the natural realm of the string quartet.

The fact that these instruments are capable of playing double notes and full chords across three and four strings—to say nothing of sub-division of parts—renders them not only melodic but also harmonic in character.[7]

From the point of view of activity and flexibility the violin takes pride of place among stringed instruments, then, in order, come the viola, 'cello and double bass. In practice the notes of extreme limit in the string quartet should be fixed as follows:

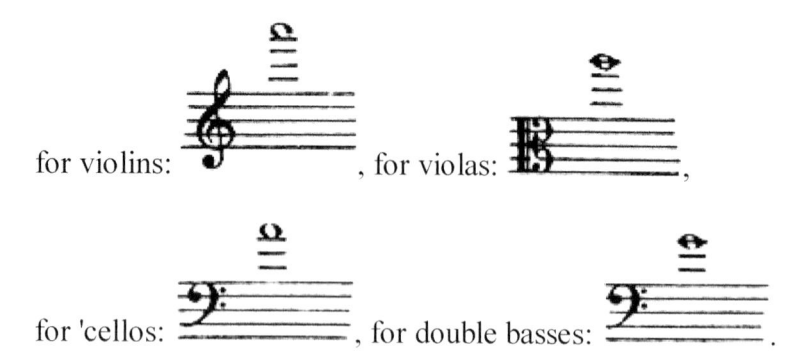

for violins: [musical notation], for violas: [musical notation],

for 'cellos: [musical notation], for double basses: [musical notation].

Higher notes given in Table A, should only be used with caution, that is to say when they are of long value, in *tremolando*, slow, flowing melodies, in not too rapid sequence of scales, and in passages of repeated notes. Skips should always be avoided.

Note. In quick passages for stringed instruments long chromatic figures are never suitable; they are difficult to play and sound indistinct and muddled. Such passages are better allotted to the wood-wind.

A limit should be set to the use of a high note on any one of the three lower strings on violins, violas and 'cellos. This note should be the one in the fourth position, either the octave note or the ninth of the open string.-9-

Nobility, warmth, and equality of tone from one end of the scale to the other are qualities common to all stringed instruments, and render them essentially superior to instruments of other groups. Further, each string has a distinctive character of its own, difficult to define in words. The top string on the violin (E) is brilliant in character, that of the viola (A) is more biting in quality and slightly nasal; the highest string on the 'cello (A) is bright and possesses a "chest-voice" timbre. The A and D strings on the violin and the D string on the violas and 'cellos are somewhat sweeter and weaker in tone than the others. Covered strings (G), on the violin (G and C), on the viola and 'cello are rather harsh. Speaking generally, the double bass is equally resonant throughout, slightly duller on the two lower strings (E and A), and more penetrating on the upper ones (D and G).

Note. Except in the case of pedal notes, the double bass rarely plays an independent part, usually moving in octaves or in unison with the 'cellos, or else doubling the bassoons. The quality of the double bass tone is therefore seldom heard by itself and the character of its different strings is not so noticeable.

The rare ability to connect sounds, or a series of sounds, the vibration of stopped strings combined with their above-named qualities—warmth and nobility of tone—renders this group of instruments far and away the best orchestral medium of melodic expression. At the same time, that portion of their range situated beyond the limits of the human voice, e.g. notes on the violin higher than the extreme top note of the soprano voice, from upwards, and notes on the double bass below the range of the bass voice, descending from

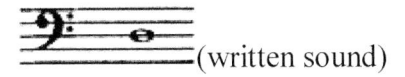

(written sound)

lose in expression and warmth of tone. Open strings are clearer and more powerful but less expressive than stopped strings.

Comparing the range of each stringed instrument with that of the human voice, we may assign: to the violin, the soprano and-10- contralto voice plus a much higher range; to the viola, the contralto and tenor voice plus a much higher register; to the 'cello, the tenor and bass voices plus a higher register; to the double bass, the bass voice plus a lower range.

The use of harmonics, the mute, and some special devices in bowing produce great difference in the resonance and tone quality of all these instruments.

Harmonics, frequently used today, alter the timbre of a stringed instrument to a very appreciable extent. Cold and transparent in soft passages, cold and brilliant in loud ones, and offering but little chance for expression, they form no fundamental part of orchestral writing, and are used simply for ornament. Owing to their lack of resonant power they should be used sparingly, and, when employed, should never be overpowered by other instruments. As a rule harmonics are employed on sustained notes, *tremolando*, or here and there for brilliant effects; they are rarely used in extremely simple melodies. Owing to a certain tonal affinity with the flute they may be said to form a kind of link between string and wood-wind instruments.

Another radical change is effected by the use of mutes. When muted, the clear, singing tone of the strings becomes dull in soft passages, turns to a slight hiss or whistle in loud ones, and the volume of tone is always greatly reduced.

The position of the bow on the string will affect the resonance of an instrument. Playing with the bow close to the bridge (*sul ponticello*), chiefly used *tremolando*, produces a metallic sound; playing on the finger-board (*sul tasto, flautando*) creates a dull, veiled effect.

Note. Another absolutely different sound results from playing with the back or wood of the bow (*col legno*). This produces a sound like a xylophone or a hollow *pizzicato*. It is discussed under the heading of instruments of little sustaining power.

Table A. String group.

(These instruments give all chromatic intervals.)

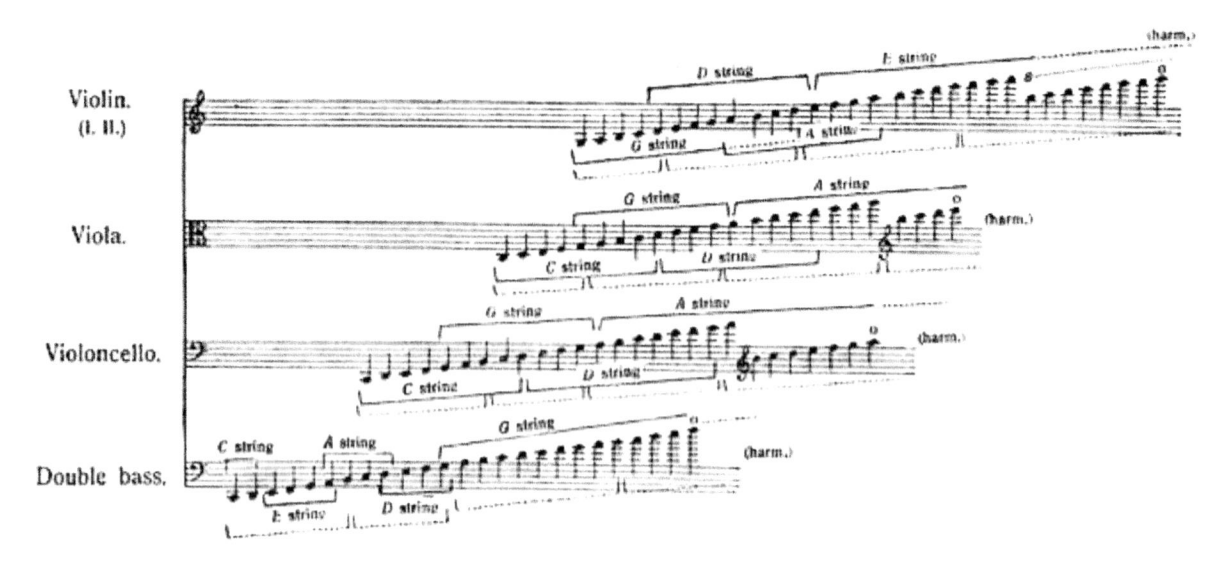

[]

Black lines on each string denote the general range in orchestral writing, the dotted lines give the registers, low, medium, high, very high.

The five sets of strings with number of players given above produce a fairly even balance of tone. If there is any surplus of strength it must be on the side of the first violins, as they must be heard distinctly on account of the important part they play in the harmonic scheme. Besides this, an extra desk of first violins is usual in all orchestras, and as a general -12- rule they possess a more powerful tone than second violins. The latter, with the violas, play a secondary part, and do not stand out so prominently. The 'cellos and double basses are heard more distinctly, and in the majority of cases form the bass in octaves.

In conclusion it may be said that the group of strings, as a melodic element, is able to perform all manner of passages, rapid and interrupted phrases of every description, diatonic or chromatic in character. Capable of sustaining notes without difficulty, of playing chords of three and four notes; adapted to the infinite variety of shades of expression, and easily divisible into numerous sundry parts, the string group in an orchestra may be considered as an harmonic element particularly rich in resource.

B. Wind instruments.

Wood-wind.

Apart from the varying number of players, the formation of the string group, with its five constituent parts remains constant, satisfying the demands of any orchestral full score. On the other hand the group of wood-wind instruments varies both as regards number of parts and the volume of tone at its command, and here the composer may choose at will. The group may be divided into three general classes: wood-wind instruments in pair's, in three's and in four's, (see table on page 13).

Arabic numerals denote the number of players on each instrument; roman figures, the parts (1st, 2nd etc.). Instruments which do not require additional players, but are taken over by one or the other executant in place of his usual instrument, are enclosed in brackets. As a rule the first flute, first oboe, first clarinet and first bassoon never change instruments; considering the importance of their parts it is not advisable for them to turn from one mouth-piece to another. The parts written for piccolo, bass flute, English horn, small clarinet, bass clarinet and double bassoon are taken by the second and third players in each group, who are more accustomed to using these instruments of a special nature.-13-

Wood-wind in pair's	Wood-wind in three's	Wood-wind in four's
(II—Piccolo).	(III—Piccolo).	1 Piccolo (IV).
2 Flutes I. II.	3 Flutes I. II. III.	3 Flutes I. II. III.
	(II—Bass flute).	(III—Bass flute).
2 Oboes I. II.	2 Oboes I. II.	3 Oboes I. II. III.
(II—Eng. horn).	1 Eng. horn (III).	1 Eng. horn (IV).
	(II—Small clarinet).	(II—Small clarinet).
2 Clarinets I. II.	3 Clarinets I. II. III.	3 Clarinets I. II. III.
(II—Bass clarinet).	(III—Bass clarinet).	1 Bass clarinet (IV).
2 Bassoons I. II.	2 Bassoons I. II.	3 Bassoons I. II. III.
	1 Double bassoon (III).	1 Double bassoon (IV).

The formation of the first class may be altered by the permanent addition of a piccolo part. Sometimes a composer writes for two piccolos or two Eng. horns etc. without increasing the original number of players required (in three's or four's).

Note I. Composers using the first class in the course of a big work (oratorio, opera, symphony, etc.) may introduce special instruments, called *extras*, for a long or short period of time; each of these instruments involves an extra player not required throughout the entire work. Meyerbeer was fond of doing this, but other composers, Glinka for example, refrain from increasing the number of performers by employing *extras* (Eng. horn part in *Rousslân*). Wagner uses all three classes in the above table (in pair's: *Tannhäuser*—in three's: *Tristan*—in four's: *The Ring*).

Note II. Mlada is the only work of mine involving formation by four's. *Ivan the Terrible, Sadko, The Legend of Tsar Saltan, The Legend of the Invisible City of Kitesh* and *The Golden Cockerel* all belong to the second class, and in my other works, wood-wind in pair's is used with a varying number of extras. *The Christmas Night*, with its two oboes, and two bassoons, three flutes and three clarinets, forms an intermediate class.

Considering the instruments it comprises, the string group offers a fair variety of colour, and contrast in compass, but this diversity of range and timbre is subtle and not easily discerned. In the wood-wind department, however, the difference in register and quality of flutes, oboes, clarinets and bassoons is striking to a degree. As a rule, wood-wind instruments are less flexible than -14- strings; they lack the vitality and power, and are less capable of different shade of expression.

In each wind instrument I have defined the *scope of greatest expression*, that is to say the range in which the instrument is best qualified to achieve the various grades of tone, (*forte, piano, cresc., dim., sforzando, morendo*, etc.)—the register which admits of the most *expressive* playing, in the truest sense of the word. Outside this range, a wind instrument is more notable for richness of colour than for expression. I am probably the originator of the term "scope of greatest expression". It does not apply to the piccolo and double bassoon which represent the two extremes of the orchestral compass. They do not possess such a register and belong to the body of highly-coloured but non-expressive instruments.

The four kinds of wind instruments: flutes, oboes, clarinets and bassoons may be generally considered to be of equal power. The same cannot be said of instruments which fulfil a special purpose: piccolo, bass flute, Eng. horn, small clarinet, bass clarinet and double bassoon. Each of these instruments has four registers: low, middle, high and extremely high, each of which is characterised by certain differences of quality and power. It is difficult to define the exact limits of each register; adjacent registers almost blend together and the passage from one to another is scarcely noticeable. But when the instrument jumps from one register to another the difference in power and quality of tone is very striking.

The four families of wind instruments may be divided into two classes: a) instruments of nasal quality and dark resonance—oboes and bassoons (Eng. horn and double bassoon); and b) instruments of "chest-voice" quality and bright tone—flutes and clarinets (piccolo, bass flute, small clarinet, bass clarinet).

These characteristics of colour and resonance—expressed in too simple and rudimentary a form—are specially noticeable in the middle and upper registers. The lower register of the oboes and bassoons is thick and rough, yet still nasal in quality; the very high compass is shrill, hard and dry. The clear resonance of the flutes and clarinets acquires something nasal and dark in the lower compass; in the very high register it becomes somewhat piercing.

Note to Table B.

In the following Table B the top note in each register serves as the bottom note in the next, as the limits to each register are not defined absolutely. The note *G* fixes the register of flutes and oboes, *C* for the clarinets and bassoons. In the very high compass those notes are only given which can really be used; anything higher and not printed as actual notes are either too difficult to produce or of no artistic value. The number of sounds obtainable in the highest compass is indefinite, and depends, partly on the quality of the instrument itself, partly on the position and application of the lips. The signs ⟩ ⟨ are not to be mistaken for *crescendo* and *diminuendo*; they indicate how the resonance of an instrument increases or diminishes in relation to the characteristic quality of its timbre. The scope of greatest expression for each typical instrument is marked thus, ⊢——⊣ under the notes; the range is the same in each instrument of the same type.

Table B. Wind group.

These instruments give all chromatic intervals.

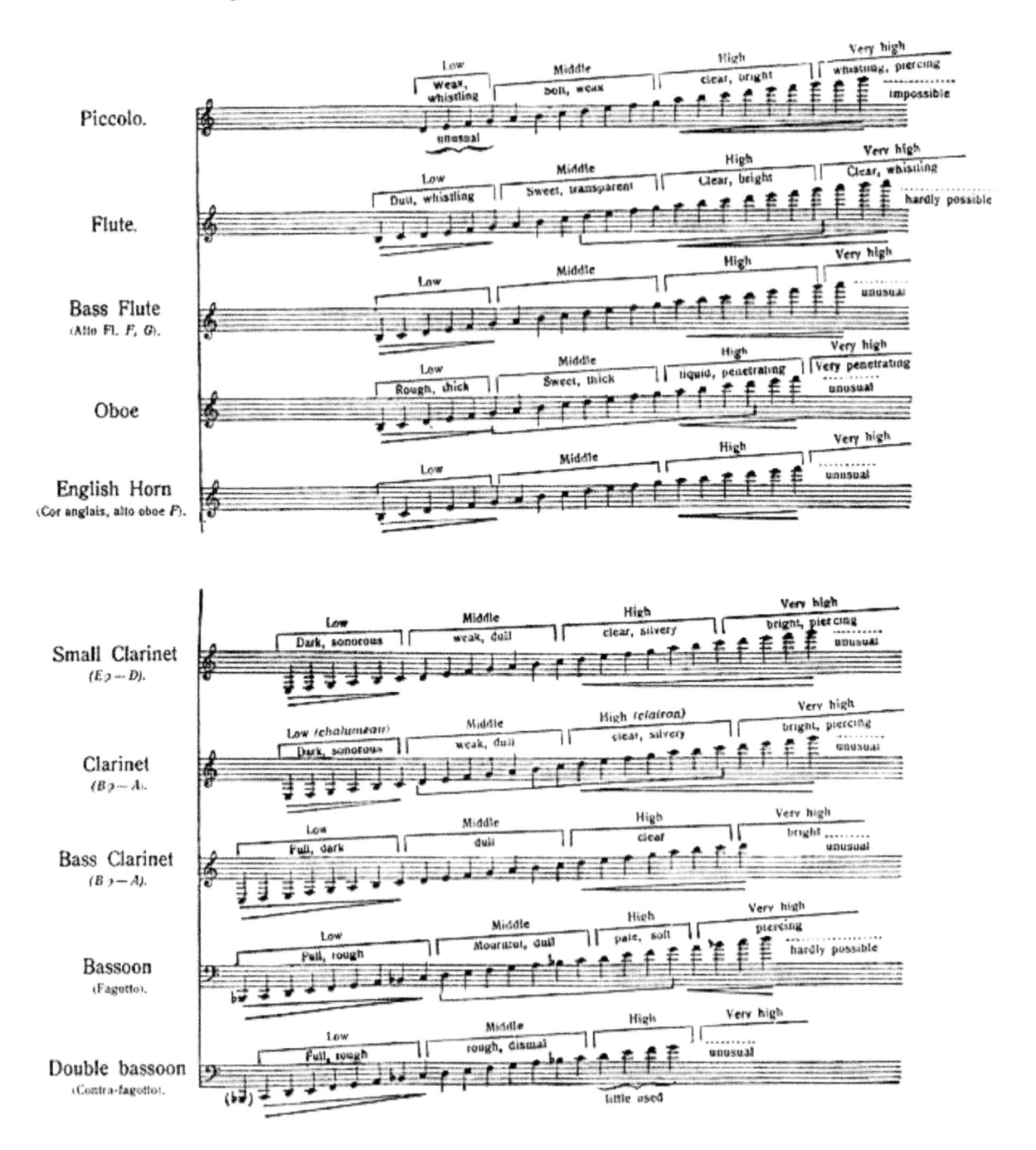

[]

Note. It is a difficult matter to define tone quality in words; we must encroach upon the domain of sight, feeling, and even taste. Though borrowed from these senses, I have no doubt as to the appropriateness of my comparisons, but, as a general rule definitions drawn from other sources are too elementary to be applied to music. No condemnatory meaning however should be attached to my descriptions, for in using the terms thick, piercing, shrill, dry, etc. my object is to express *artistic* fitness in words, rather than material exactitude. Instrumental sounds which have no musical meaning are classed by me in the category of *useless sounds*, and I refer to them as such, giving my reasons. With the exception of these, the reader is advised to consider all other orchestral timbres beautiful from an artistic point of view, although it is necessary, at times, to put them to other uses.

Further on, a <u>table of wind instruments</u> is appended, outlining the approximate limit of range, defining different qualities of tone and indicating the scope of greatest expression (the piccolo and double bassoon excepted).

Flutes and clarinets are the most flexible wood-wind instruments (the flutes in particular), but for expressive power and subtlety in *nuances* the clarinet supersedes them; this instrument can reduce volume of tone to a mere breath. The nasal instruments, oboe and bassoon, are less mobile and supple; this is accounted for by their double reed, but, having to effect all sorts of scales and rapid passages in common with the flutes and clarinets, oboes and bassoons may be considered melodic instruments in the real sense of the word, only of a more *cantabile* and peaceful character. In very quick passages they often double the flutes, clarinets or strings.

The four families are equally capable of *legato* and *staccato* playing and changing from one to the other in different ways, but distinct and penetrating *staccato* passages are better suited to the oboes and bassoons, while the flutes and clarinets excel in well-sustained *legato* phrases. Composite *legato* passages should be allotted to the first two instruments, composite *staccato* passages to the latter pair, but these general directions should not deter the orchestrator from adopting the opposite plan.

In comparing the technical individualities of the wood-wind the following fundamental differences should be noted:

a) The rapid repetition of a single note by single tonguing is common to all wind instruments; repetition of a single note by means of double tonguing is only possible on the flute, a reedless instrument.

b) On account of its construction the clarinet is not well adapted to sudden leaps from one octave to another; these skips are easier on flutes, oboes and bassoons.-19-

c) *Arpeggios* and rapid alternation of two intervals *legato* sound well on flutes and clarinets, but not on oboes and bassoons.

Wood-wind players cannot manage extremely long sustained passages, as they are compelled to take breath; care must be taken therefore to give them a little rest from time to time. This is unnecessary in the case of string players.

In the endeavour to characterise the timbre of each instrument typical of the four families, from a psychological point of view, I do not hesitate to make the following general remarks which apply generally to the middle and upper registers of each instrument:

a) Flute.—Cold in quality, specially suitable, in the major key, to melodies of light and graceful character; in the minor key, to slight touches of transient sorrow.

b) Oboe.—Artless and gay in the major, pathetic and sad in the minor.

c) Clarinet.—Pliable and expressive, suitable, in the major, to melodies of a joyful or contemplative character, or to outbursts of mirth; in the minor, to sad and reflective melodies or impassioned and dramatic passages.

d) Bassoon.—In the major, an atmosphere of senile mockery; a sad, ailing quality in the minor.

In the extreme registers these instruments convey the following impressions to my mind:

	Low register	*Very high register*
a) Flute—	Dull, cold	Brilliant
b) Oboe—	Wild	Hard, dry
c) Clarinet—	Ringing, threatening	Piercing
d) Bassoon—	Sinister	Tense.

Note. It is true that no mood or frame of mind, whether it be joyful or sad, meditative or lively, careless or reflective, mocking or distressed can be aroused by one single isolated timbre; it depends more upon the general melodic line, the harmony, rhythm, and dynamic shades of expression, upon the whole formation of a given piece of music. The choice of instruments and timbre to be adopted depends on the position which melody and harmony occupy in the seven-octave scale of the orchestra; for example, a melody of light character in the tenor register could not be given to the flutes, or a sad, plaintive phrase in the high soprano register confided to the bassoons. But the ease with which tone colour can be adapted to expression must not be forgotten, and in the first of these two cases it may be conceded that the mocking character of the bassoon could easily and quite naturally assume a light-hearted aspect, and-20- in the second case, that the slightly melancholy timbre of the flute is somewhat related to the feeling of sorrow and distress with which the passage is to be permeated. The case of a melody coinciding in character with the instrument on which it is played is of special importance, as the effect produced cannot fail to be successful. There are also moments when a composer's artistic feeling prompts him to employ instruments, the character of which is at variance with the written melody (for eccentric, grotesque effects, etc.).

The following remarks illustrate the characteristics, timbre, and employment of special instruments:

The duty of the piccolo and small clarinet is, principally, to extend the range of the ordinary flute and clarinet in the high register. The whistling, piercing quality of the piccolo in its highest compass is extraordinarily powerful, but does not lend itself to more moderate shades of expression. The small clarinet in its highest register is more penetrating than the ordinary clarinet. The low and middle range of the piccolo and small clarinet correspond to the same register in the normal flute and clarinet, but the tone is so much weaker that it is of little service in those regions. The double bassoon extends the range of the ordinary bassoon in the low register. The characteristics of the bassoon's low compass are still further accentuated in the corresponding range of the double bassoon, but the middle and upper registers of the latter are by no means so useful. The very deep notes of the double bassoon are remarkably thick and dense in quality, very powerful in *piano* passages.

Note. Nowadays, when the limits of the orchestral scale are considerably extended (up to the high *C* of the 7th octave, and down to the low *C*, 16 ft. contra octave), the piccolo forms an indispensable constituent of the wind-group; similarly, it is recognised that the double bassoon is capable of supplying valuable assistance. The small clarinet is rarely employed and only for colour effects.

The English horn, or alto oboe (oboe in *F*) is similar in tone to the ordinary oboe, the listless, dreamy quality of its timbre being sweet in the extreme. In the low register it is fairly penetrating. The bass clarinet, though strongly resembling the ordinary clarinet, is of darker colour in the low register and lacks the silvery quality in the upper notes; it is incapable of joyful expression. The bass flute is an instrument seldom used even today; it possesses the same features as the flute, but it is colder in-21- colour, and crystalline in the middle and high regions. These three particular instruments, apart from extending the low registers of the instruments to which they belong, have their own distinctive peculiarities of timbre, and are often used in the orchestra, as solo instruments, clearly exposed.

Note. Of the six special instruments referred to above, the piccolo and double bassoon were the first to be used in the orchestra; the latter, however, was neglected after Beethoven's death and did not reappear until towards the end of the 19th century. The Eng. horn and bass clarinet were employed initially during the first half of the same century by Berlioz, Meyerbeer, and others, and for some time retained their position as *extras*, to become, later on, permanent orchestral factors, first in the theatre, then in the concert room. Very few attempts have been made to introduce the small clarinet into the orchestra (Berlioz etc.); this instrument together with the bass flute is used in my opera-ballet *Mlada* (1892), and also in my most recent compositions, *The Christmas Night*, and

Sadko; the bass flute will also be found in *The Legend of the Invisible City of Kitesh*, and in the revised version of "*Ivan the Terrible*".

Of late years the habit of muting the wood-wind has come into fashion. This is done by inserting a soft pad, or a piece of rolled-up cloth into the bell of the instrument. Mutes deaden the tone of oboes, Eng. horns, and bassoons to such an extent that it is possible for these instruments to attain the extreme limit of *pianissimo* playing. The muting of clarinets is unnecessary, as they can play quite softly enough without artificial means. It has not yet been discovered how to mute the flutes; such a discovery would render great service to the piccolo. The lowest notes on the bassoon,

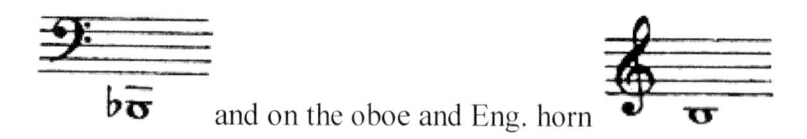

and on the oboe and Eng. horn

are impossible when the instruments are muted. Mutes have no effect in the highest register of wind instruments.

Brass.

The formation of the group of brass instruments, like that of the wood-wind is not absolutely uniform, and varies in different scores. The brass group may be divided into three general classes corresponding to those of the wood-wind (in pair's, in three's, and in four's).-22-

Group corresponding to the wood-wind in pair's	Group corresponding to the wood-wind in three's	Group corresponding to the wood-wind in four's
2 Trumpets I, II.	3 Trumpets I, II, III. (III—Alto trumpet or: { 2 Cornets I, II. { 2 Trumpets I, II.)	(II—Small trumpet). 3 Trumpets I, II, III. (III—Alto trumpet or Bass trumpet.)
4 Horns I, II, III, IV.	4 Horns I, II, III, IV.	6 or 8 Horns I, II, III, IV, V, VI, VII, VIII.
3 Trombones.	3 Trombones I, II, III.	3 Trombones I, II, III.
1 Tuba.	1 Tuba[8].	1 Tuba.

The directions are the same as in the preceding table for wood-wind. It is evident that in all three classes the formation may vary as the composer wishes. In music for the theatre or concert room page after page may be written without the use of trumpets, trombones and tuba, or some instrument may be introduced, temporarily as an *extra*. In the above table I have given the most typical formations, and those which are the most common at the present day.

Note I. Besides the instruments given above, Richard Wagner used some others in *The Ring*, notably the quartet of tenor and bass tubas, and a contrabass trombone. Sometimes these additions weigh too heavily on the other groups, and at other times they render the rest of the brass ineffective. For this reason composers have doubtless refrained from employing such instruments, and Wagner himself did not include them in the score of *Parsifal*. Some present-day composers (Richard Strauss, Scriabine) write for as many as five trumpets.

Note II. From the middle of the 19th century onward the natural brass disappeared from the orchestra, giving place to valve instruments. In my second opera, *The May Night* I used natural horns and trumpets, changing the keys, and writing the best notes "stopped"; this was purposely done for practise.

Though far less flexible than the wood-wind, brass instruments heighten the effect of other orchestral groups by their powerful resonance. Trumpets, trombones, and tubas are about equal in-23- strength; cornets have not quite the same force; horns, in *forte* passages, are about one half as strong, but *piano*, they have the same weight as other brass instruments played softly. To obtain an equal balance, therefore, the marks of expression in the horns should be one degree stronger than in the rest of the brass; if the trumpets and trombones play *pp*, the horns should be marked *p*. On the other hand, to obtain a proper balance in *forte* passages, two horns are needed to one trumpet or one trombone.

Brass instruments are so similar in range and timbre that the discussion of register is unnecessary. As a general rule quality becomes more brilliant as the higher register is approached, and *vice versa*, with a decrease in tone. Played *pp* the resonance is sweet; played *ff* the tone is hard and "crackling". Brass instruments possess a remarkable capacity for swelling from *pianissimo* to *fortissimo*, and reducing the tone inversely, the *sf* ⟹ *p* effect being excellent.

The following remarks as to character and tone quality may be added:

a) 1. *Trumpets* (B♭ -A). Clear and fairly penetrating in tone, stirring and rousing in *forte* passages; in *piano* phrases the high notes are full and silvery, the low notes troubled, as though threatening danger.

2. *Alto trumpet* (in F). An instrument of my own invention, first used by me in the opera-ballet *Mlada*. In the deep register (notes 2 to 3 in the trumpet scale) it possesses a fuller, clearer, and finer tone. Two ordinary trumpets with an alto trumpet produce greater

smoothness and equality in resonance than three ordinary trumpets. Satisfied with the beauty and usefulness of the alto trumpet, I have consistently written for it in my later works, combined with wood-wind in three's.

Note. To obviate the difficulty of using the alto trumpet in ordinary theatres and some concert rooms, I have not brought into play the last four notes of its lowest register or their neighbouring chromatics; by this means the alto trumpet part may be played by an ordinary trumpet in $B\flat$ or A.

3. *Small trumpet* (in $E\flat$ -D). Invented by me and used for the first time in *Mlada* to realise the very high-24- trumpet notes without difficulty. In tonality and range the instrument is similar to the soprano cornet in a military band.

Note. The small trumpet, ($B\flat$ -A) sounding an octave higher than the ordinary trumpet has not yet appeared in musical literature.

b) *Cornets* (in $B\flat$ -A). Possessing a quality of tone similar to the trumpet, but softer and weaker. It is a beautiful instrument though rarely employed today in theatre or concert room. Expert players can imitate the cornet tone on the trumpet, and *vice versa*.

c) *Horn* (in F). The tone of this instrument is soft, poetical, and full of beauty. In the lower register it is dark and brilliant; round and full in the upper. The middle notes resemble those of the bassoon and the two instruments blend well together. The horn, therefore, serves as a link between the brass and wood-wind. In spite of valves the horn has but little mobility and would seem to produce its tone in a languid and lazy manner.

d) *Trombone.* Dark and threatening in the deepest register, brilliant and triumphant in the high compass. The *piano* is full but somewhat heavy, the *forte* powerful and sonorous. Valve trombones are more mobile than slide trombones, but the latter are certainly to be preferred as regards nobility and equality of sound, the more so from the fact that these instruments are rarely required to perform quick passages, owing to the special character of their tone.

e) *Tuba.* Thick and rough in quality, less characteristic than the trombone, but valuable for the strength and beauty of its low notes. Like the double bass and double bassoon, the tuba is eminently useful for doubling, an octave lower, the bass of the group to which it belongs. Thanks to its valves, the tuba is fairly flexible.

Table C. Brass group.

These instruments give all chromatic intervals.[A] [B]

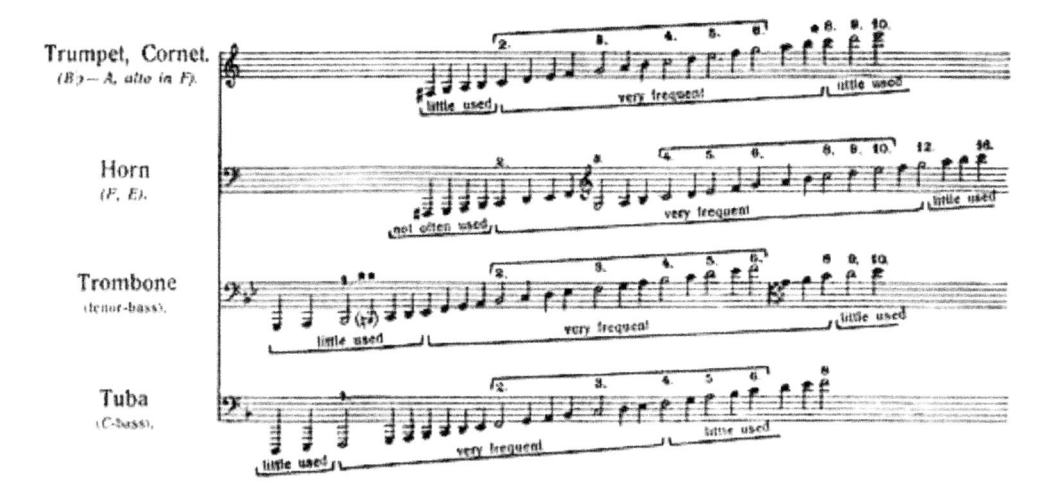

[]

Natural sounds are given in white notes. The upper lines indicate the scope of greatest expression.

The group of brass instruments, though uniform in resonance throughout its constituent parts, is not so well adapted to expressive playing (in the exact sense of the word) as the wood-wind group. Nevertheless, a scope of greatest expression may be distinguished-26--25- in the middle registers. In company with the piccolo and double bassoon it is not given to the small trumpet (*Eb -D*) and tuba to play with any great amount of expression. The rapid and rhythmical repetition of a note by single tonguing is possible to all members of the brass, but double tonguing can only be done on instruments with a small mouth-piece, trumpets and cornets. These two instruments can execute rapid *tremolando* without difficulty. The remarks on breathing, in the section devoted to the wood-wind, apply with equal force to the brass.

The use of stopped notes and mutes alters the character of brass tone. Stopped notes can only be employed on trumpets, cornets and horns; the shape of trombones and tubas prevents the hand from being inserted into the bell. Though mutes are applied indiscriminately to all brass instruments in the orchestra, tubas rarely possess them. Stopped and muted notes are similar in quality. On the trumpet, muting a note produces a better tone than stopping it.

In the horn both methods are employed; single notes are stopped in short phrases, muted in longer ones. I do not propose to describe the difference between the two operations in detail, and will leave the reader to acquire the knowledge for himself, and to form an opinion as to its importance from his own personal observation. Sufficient to say that the tone is deadened by both methods, assuming a wild "crackling" character in *forte* passages, tender and dull in *piano*. Resonance is greatly reduced, the silvery tone of the instrument so lost and a timbre resembling that of the oboe and Eng. horn is approached. Stopped notes (*con sordino*) are marked + underneath the note, sometimes followed by ○, denoting the resumption of open sounds, *senza sordini*. Brass instruments, when muted, produce an effect of distance.

C. Instruments of little sustaining power.

Plucked strings.

When the usual orchestral string quartet (Vns I, Vns II, Violas, 'Cellos, D. basses) does not make use of the bow, but plucks the strings with the finger, it becomes to my mind a new and inde-27-pendent group with its own particular quality of tone. Associated with the harp, which produces sound in a similar manner, I consider it separately under the heading of plucked strings.

Note. In this group may be classed the guitar, zither, balalaïka; instruments plucked with a quill, such as the domra,[9] the mandoline etc., all of which may be used in an orchestra, but have no place in the scope of the present book.

Pizzicato.

Although capable of every degree of power from *ff* to *pp*, *pizzicato* playing has but small range of expression, and is used chiefly as a colour effect. On open strings it is resonant and heavy, on stopped strings shorter and duller; in the high positions it is rather dry and hard.

Table D on page 31 indicates the range in which *pizzicato* may be used on each stringed instrument.

In the orchestra, *pizzicato* comes into operation in two distinct ways: a) on single notes, b) on double notes and chords. The fingers of the right hand playing *pizz.* are far less agile than the bow; *pizz.* passages therefore can never be performed as quickly as those played *arco*. Moreover, the speed of *pizzicato* playing depends upon the thickness of the strings; on the double basses, for instance, it must always be much slower than on the violins.

In *pizzicato* chords it is better to avoid open strings, which produce a more brilliant tone than of covered strings. Chords of four notes allow of greater freedom and vigour of attack, as there is no danger of accidentally touching a wrong note. Natural harmonics played *pizz.* create a charming effect; the tone is weak however, and they are chiefly successful on the violoncello.

Harp.

In the orchestra, the harp is almost entirely an harmonic or accompanying instrument. The majority of scores require only one harp part, but in recent times composers have written for two or even three harps, which are sometimes compressed into the one part.-28-

Note. Full orchestras should include three or even four harps. My operas *Sadko*, *The Legend of the Invisible City of Kitesh*, and *The Golden Cockerel* are designed for two harps, *Mlada* for three.

The special function of the harp lies in the execution of chords, and the florid figures springing from them. As only four notes at the most can be played by each hand, the notes of a chord should be written close together, with not too great a space between one hand and the other. The chords must always be broken (*arpeggiato*); should the composer wish otherwise he should notify it (*non arpeggiato*). In the middle and lower octaves the resonance of the strings is slightly prolonged, and dies away gradually. In changes of harmony the player stops the vibration of the strings with his hands, but, in quick modulations, this method is not feasible, and the mixture of one chord with another produces a discordant effect. It follows that more or less rapid figures can only be realised clearly and neatly in the upper register of the harp, where the strings are shorter and harder in tone.

As a general rule, in the whole range of the harp:

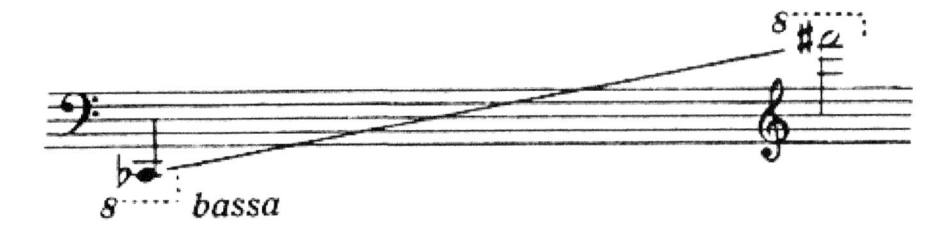

only the notes of the first to the fourth octave are used; the extreme notes in both compasses may be employed in special circumstances, and for doubling in octaves.

The harp is essentially a diatonic instrument, since all chromatic passages depend on the manipulation of the pedals. For this reason the harp does not lend itself to rapid modulation, and the orchestrator is advised to bear this fact in mind. But the difficulty may be obviated by using two harps alternately.[10]

Note. I would remind the reader that the harp is not capable of double sharps or double flats. For this reason, certain modulations from one key to another one, adjacent to it can only be accomplished enharmonically. For instance, the transition from *C* flat, *G* flat or *D* flat, major to their minor subdominant chords or keys is not possible owing to double flats. It is therefore-29- necessary to start enharmonically from the keys of *B*, *F* sharp or *C* sharp, major. Similarly, on account of double sharps, it is impossible to change from *A* sharp, *D* sharp or *G* sharp, minor to their respective dominant major chords or keys; *B* flat, *E* flat and *A* flat, minor must be the starting-points.

The technical operation known as *glissando* is peculiar to the harp alone. Taking for granted that the reader is conversant with the methods of acquiring different scales by means of double-notched pedals, it will be sufficient to remark that *glissando* scales produce a discordant medley of sound owing to the length of time the strings continue to vibrate, and therefore, as a *purely musical* effect, *glissando* can only be used in the upper octaves, quite *piano*, where the sound of the strings is sufficiently clear, yet not too prolonged. *Forte glissando* scales, entailing the use of the lower and middle strings are only permissible as embellishments. Glissando passages in chords of the seventh and ninth, enharmonically obtained, are much more common, and as the above reservations do not apply, every dynamic shade of tone is possible. Chords in harmonics can only consist of three notes written close together, two for the left hand and one for the right.

The tender poetic quality of the harp is adapted to every dynamic shade, but it is never a very powerful instrument, and the orchestrator should treat it with respect.

At least three, if not four harps in unison are necessary, if they are to be heard against a full orchestra playing *forte*. The more rapidly a *glissando* passage is played, the louder it will sound. Harmonic notes on the harp have great charm but little resonance, and are only possible played quite softly. Speaking generally, the harp, like the string quartet, *pizzicato*, is more an instrument of colour than expression.

Percussion instruments producing determinate sounds, keyed instruments.

Kettle-drums.

Kettle-drums, indispensable to every theatre and concert orchestra occupy the most important place in the group of percussion instruments. A pair of kettle-drums (*Timpani*), in the tonic and dominant keys, was the necessary attribute of an orchestra up to, and -30- including Beethoven's time, but, from the middle of the 19th century onward, in western Europe and in Russia, an ever-increasing need was felt for the presence of three or even four kettle-drums, during the whole course or part of a work. If the expensive chromatic drum, permitting instant tuning is rarely met with, still, in the majority of good orchestras, three screw drums are generally to be found. The composer can therefore take it for granted that a good timpanist, having three kettle-drums at his command, will be able to tune at least one of them during a pause of some length.

The limits of possible change in Beethoven's time was considered to be:

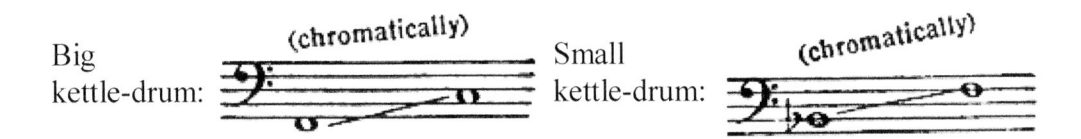

Big kettle-drum: (chromatically)   Small kettle-drum: (chromatically)

In these days it is difficult to define the precise extent of high compass in the kettle-drums, as this depends entirely on the size and quality of the smallest one, of which there are many kinds, but I advise the composer to select:

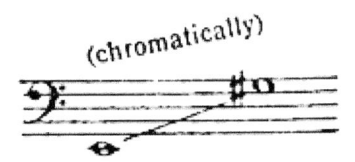

(chromatically)

Note. A magnificent kettle-drum of very small size was made for my opera-ballet *Mlada*; this instrument gave the $D\flat$ of the fourth octave.

Kettle-drums are capable of every dynamic shade of tone, from thundering *fortissimo* to a barely perceptible *pianissimo*. In *tremolando* they can execute the most gradual *crescendo, diminuendo*, the *sfp* and *morendo*.

To deaden the sound, a piece of cloth is generally placed on the skin of the drum, according to the instruction: *timpani coperti* (muffled drums).

Table D.

Pizzicato.

Violin.

Viola.

Violoncello.

Double bass.

[]

The black notes are dry and hard, without resonance, and should only be used when doubled with the wood-wind.

* Table E.

Glockenspiel, celesta, xylophone.

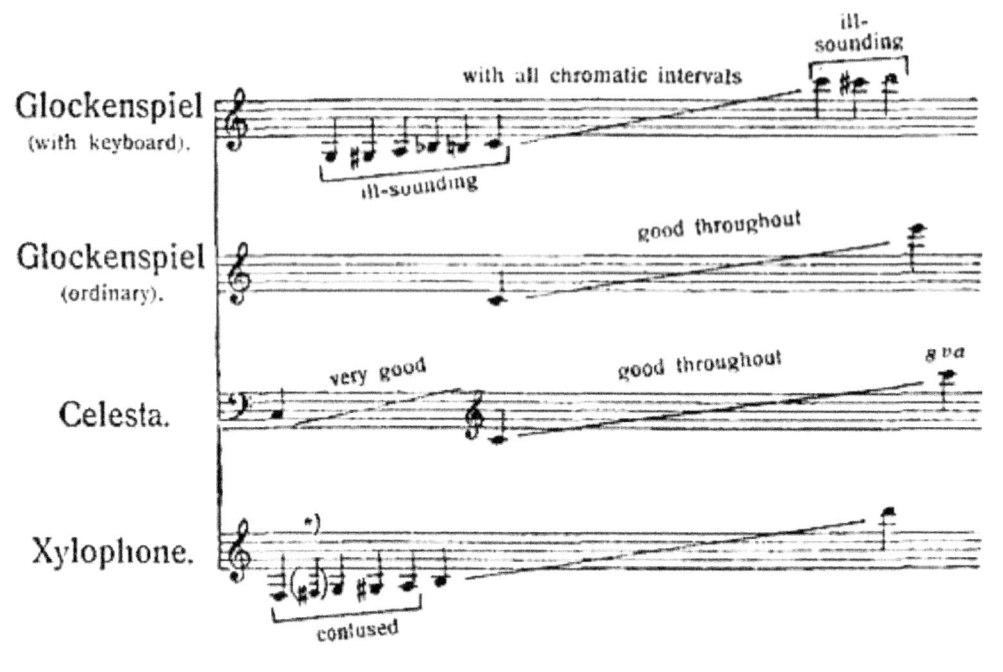

[]

Piano and Celesta.

The use of a piano in the orchestra (apart from pianoforte concertos) belongs almost entirely to the Russian school.[11] The object is two-fold: the quality of tone, either alone, or combined with-32- that of the harp, is made to imitate a popular instrument, the guzli, (as in Glinka), or a soft peal of bells. When the piano forms part of an orchestra, not as a solo instrument, an upright is preferable to a grand, but today the piano is gradually being superseded by the celesta, first used by Tschaikovsky. In the celesta, small steel plates take the place of strings, and the hammers falling on them produce a delightful sound, very similar to the *glockenspiel*. The celesta is only found in full orchestras; when it is not available it should be replaced by an upright piano, and not the *glockenspiel*.

Glockenspiel, Bells, Xylophone.

The *glockenspiel* (*campanelli*) may be made of steel bars, or played with a keyboard. The first type is the more satisfactory and possesses greater resonance. The use of the *glockenspiel* is similar to the celesta, but its tone is more brilliant and penetrating. Big bells in the shape of hollow discs or metal tubes,[12] or real church bells of moderate size may be considered more as theatrical properties than orchestral instruments.

The xylophone is a species of harmonica composed of strips or cylinders of wood, struck with two little hammers. It produces a clattering sound, both powerful and piercing.

To complete this catalogue of sounds mention should be made of the strings playing *col legno*, that is with the wood or back of the bow. The sound produced is similar to the xylophone, and gains in quality as the number of players is increased.

A table is appended showing the range of the celesta, *glockenspiel* and xylophone.

Percussion instruments producing indefinite sounds.

Instruments in this group, such as triangle, castanets, little bells, tambourine, switch or rod (*Rute*. Ger.), side or military drum, cymbals, bass drum, and Chinese gong do not take any harmonic or melodic part in the orchestra, and can only be considered as ornamental instruments pure and simple. They have no intrinsic-33- musical meaning, and are just mentioned by the way. The first three may be considered as *high*, the four following as *medium*, and the last *two* as deep instruments. This may serve as a guide to their use with percussion instruments of determinate sounds, playing in corresponding registers.

Comparison of resonance in orchestral groups and combination of different tone qualities.

In comparing the resonance of the respective groups of sound-sustaining instruments we arrive at the following approximate conclusions:

In the most resonant group, the brass, the strongest instruments are the trumpets, trombones and tuba. In loud passages the horns are only one-half as strong, 1 Trumpet = 1 Trombone = 1 Tuba = 2 Horns. Wood-wind instruments, in *forte* passages, are twice as weak as the horns, 1 Horn = 2 Clarinets = 2 Oboes = 2 Flutes = 2 Bassoons; but, in *piano* passages, all wind-instruments, wood or brass are of fairly equal balance.

It is more difficult to establish a comparison in resonance between wood-wind and strings, as everything depends on the number of the latter, but, in an orchestra of medium formation, it may be taken for granted that in *piano* passages, the whole of one department (*all* 1st Violins or *all* 2nd Violins etc.) is equivalent in strength to one wind instrument, (Violins I = 1 Flute etc.), and, in *forte* passages, to two wind instruments, (Violins I = 2 Flutes = 1 Oboe + 1 Clarinet, etc.).

It is still harder to form a comparison with instruments of little sustaining power, for too great a diversity in production and emission of sound exists. The combined force of groups of sustained resonance easily overpowers the strings played *pizz.* or *col legno*, the piano played softly, or the celesta. As regards the *glockenspiel*, bells, and xylophone, their emphatic tone will easily prevail over other groups in combination. The same may be said of the kettle-drums with their ringing, resounding quality, and also of other subsidiary instruments.

The influence of the timbre of one group on another is noticeable when the groups are doubled; for instance, when the wood-wind timbre is closely allied to the strings on the one hand, and to the brass on the other. Re-inforcing both, the wind *thickens* the strings- 34- and *softens* the brass. The strings do not blend so well with the brass, and when the two groups are placed side by side, each is heard too distinctly. The combination of the three different timbres in unison produces a rich, mellow and coherent tone.

All, or several wind instruments in combination will absorb one department of added strings:

    2 Fl. + 2 Ob. + Vns I,
or: 2 Ob. + 2 Cl. + Violas,
or: 2 Cl. + 2 Fag. + 'Cellos.

One department of strings added to the wood-wind in unison produces a sweet coherent quality, the wood-wind timbre still predominating; but the addition of one wind instrument to all or part of the strings in unison, only thickens the resonance of the latter, the wood-wind timbre being lost in the process:

    Vns I + Vns II + 1 Ob.,
or: Violas + 'Cellos + 1 Cl.
or: 'Cellos + D. basses + 1 Fag.

Muted strings do not combine so well with wood-wind, as the two tone qualities remain distinct and separate. Uniting plucked strings and percussion with instruments of sustained resonance results in the following: wind instruments, wood and brass, strengthen and clarify *pizzicato* strings, harp, kettle-drums and percussion generally, the latter lending a touch of relief to the tone of the wood-wind. Uniting plucked strings and percussion with bowed instruments does not produce such a satisfactory blend, both qualities being heard independently. The combination of plucked strings with percussion alone, is excellent; the two blend perfectly, and the consequent increase in resonance yields an admirable effect.

The relationship which exists between string harmonics and the flute or piccolo constitutes a link between the two groups in the upper range of the orchestra. Moreover, the timbre of the viola may be vaguely compared to the middle register of the bassoon and the lowest compass of the clarinet; hence, in the medium orchestral range, a point of contact is established between the quartet of strings and the wood-wind.

The bassoon and horn provide the connection between wood-wind and brass, these two instruments being somewhat analogous-35- in character when played *piano* or *mezzo-forte*; the flute also, in its lowest register, recalls the *pianissimo* trumpet tone. Stopped and muted notes in horns and trumpets are similar in quality to the oboe and Eng. horn, and blend tolerably well with the latter instrument.

Concluding this survey of orchestral groups I add a few remarks which seem to me of special importance.

The principal part in music is undertaken by three instrumental groups of sustained resonance, representing the three primary elements, melody, harmony and rhythm. Instruments of little sustaining power, though sometimes used independently, are chiefly employed for ornament and colour; instruments producing indeterminate sounds play no melodic or harmonic part, their functions being purely rhythmical.

By glancing at the order in which the six orchestral groups are placed, strings, wood-wind, brass, plucked strings, percussion producing definite, and those producing indefinite sounds, the reader will be able to determine the part played by each in the art of orchestration, from the secondary standpoint of colour and expression. As regards expression, the strings come first, and the expressive capacity of the other groups diminishes in the above order, colour being the only attribute of the last group of percussion instruments.

The same order obtains from the standpoint of general effect in orchestration. We can listen to strings for an almost indefinite period of time without getting tired, so varied are their characteristics (*vide* the number of string quartets, suites, serenades etc. written for strings alone). The addition of a single group of strings will add lustre to a passage for wind instruments. On the other hand, the quality of wind instruments soon becomes wearisome; the same may be said of plucked strings, and also percussion of every kind which should only be employed at reasonable intervals in orchestral composition.

It cannot be denied that the constant use of compound timbres, in pair's, in three's etc. eliminates characteristics of tone, and produces a dull, neutral texture, whereas the employment of simple, elementary combinations gives infinitely greater scope for variety in colour.

7 (20) June 1908.

Chapter II.

MELODY.

Whether it be long or short, a simple theme or a melodic phrase, melody should always stand out in relief from the accompaniment. This may be done by artificial or natural means; artificially, when the question of tone quality does not come into consideration, and the melody is detached by means of strongly accentuated dynamic shades; naturally, by selection and contrast of timbres, strengthening of resonance by doubling, tripling, etc., or crossing of parts (violoncellos above the violas and violins, clarinets or oboes above the flutes, bassoons above the clarinets etc.).

Melody planned in the upper parts stands out from the very fact of position alone, and likewise, to a less degree when it is situated in the low register. In the middle of the orchestral range it is not so prominent and the methods referred to above come into operation. They may also be employed for two part melody (in thirds and sixths) and for polyphonic writing.

Melody in stringed instruments.

Instances of the melodic use of stringed instruments are innumerable. The reader will find many examples in the present treatise. With the exception of the double basses,—dull in tone and of little flexibility, chiefly employed in unison or in octaves with the violoncellos,—each of the other stringed instruments, taken independently, is qualified to assume full responsibility for the melodic line.

a) Violins.

Melody in the soprano-alto register and an extra-high compass usually falls to the lot of the 1st Violins, sometimes to the 2nd Violins or to both in unison, a process which produces fuller resonance without impairing quality of tone.

Examples:

The Tsar's Bride 84.[C]—*Pianissimo* melody (Vns I) of a -37-troubled dramatic character. Harmonic accompaniment (Vns II and Violas *tremolando*—middle parts; the Violoncellos forming the bass).

Antar, before 70.—Descending melodic phrase, Vns I *con sordini piano*.

No. 1. *Shéhérazade* 2nd movement B. A *piano* melody (Vns I) graceful in character.

Antar 12. Light graceful melody, oriental in style; a dance measure (Vns I *con sord.*), the mutes producing a dull ethereal quality of tone.

No. 2. *The Legend of the Invisible City of Kitesh* 283.

No. 3. *Spanish Capriccio* J. Vns I in the upper register doubling the high register of the wood-wind. Choice resonance.

b) Violas.

Melody in the alto-tenor register and a still higher compass is assigned to the violas. *Cantabile* melodies however are not so frequently written for violas as for violins and 'cellos, partly because the viola tone is slightly nasal in quality and better fitted for short characteristic phrases, partly because the number of viola players in an orchestra is smaller. Melodies confided to the violas are generally doubled by other strings or by the wood-wind.

Examples:

No. 4. *Pan Voyevoda*, duet in Act II 145. A long *cantabile* melody in the violas, *dolce*, in unison with the *mezzo soprano* voice.

No. 5. *The Golden Cockerel* 193.—Flowing *cantabile*.

No. 6. *Sadko.* Symphonic tableau 12.—Muted violas. A short dance theme, *piano* in $D\flat$ major. (The same theme in Eng. horn-38- in the 6th scene of the opera *Sadko* is slightly more penetrating in tone).

c) Violoncellos.

Violoncellos, representing the tenor-bass range + an extra-high compass are more often entrusted with tense passionate *cantabile* melody than with distinctive figures or rapid phrases. Such melodies are usually laid out for the top string (A) which possesses a wonderfully rich "chest" quality.

Examples:

Antar 56. *Cantabile* on the *A* string.

Antar 63. The same melody in $D\flat$ maj. on the *D* string (doubled by the bassoons).

No. 7. *Pan Voyevoda* 134, nocturne, "Moonlight". A broad melody *dolce ed espressivo*, afterwards doubled by the first violins an octave higher.

No. 8. *Snegourotchka* 231. At the fifth bar, a melody on the *A* string *cantabile ed espressivo*, imitating the first clarinet.

No. 9. *Snegourotchka* 274. Melodic phrase with embellishments.

d) Double basses.

Owing to its register—*basso profondo* + a still lower compass,—and its muffled resonance, the double bass is little capable of broad *cantabile* phrases and only in unison or in octaves with the 'cellos. In my own compositions there is no phrase of any importance given to the double bass without the support of 'cellos or bassoons.

Examples:

* No. 10. *Legend of Kitesh* 306. Double bass solo, doubled first by the double bassoon, later by the bassoon. This example affords an instance of the rare use of the alto clef (in the last few notes).

* No. 11. *The Golden Cockerel* 120.—D. basses + D. bassoons.-39-

Grouping in unison.

a) Vns I + Vns II.—It goes without saying that this combination entails no alteration in colour; it gains in power and richness of tone by reason of the increased number of players, and is usually attended by doubling of the melody in some departments of the wood-wind. The large number of violins prevents the wood-wind predominating, and the tone quality remains that of the string quartet, enriched and amplified.

Examples:

No. 12. *Shéhérazade*, beginning of the third movement. *Cantabile* for Vns I and II on the *D* string, then on the *A*.

The May Night, overture D. Quick *piano* melody, beginning *cantabile* and divided later in octaves

$\genfrac{(}{)}{0pt}{}{\text{Vns I}}{\text{Vns II}}{8)}$

with florid embellishment.

No. 13. *The Golden Cockerel* 170.—Vns I + II muted.

b) Violins + Violas.—The combination of violins and violas presents no special characteristics, as in the preceding case. The violins remain predominant, and the resonance is rich and full.

Examples:

No. 14. *Sadko* 208.—Vns I + II + Violas (*G* string). Quiet *cantabile* melody *pp*, in unison with the altos and tenors of the chorus.

The *Golden Cockerel* 142.—Same combination.

c) Violas + 'Cellos.—Produces a rich full resonance, the 'cello quality predominating.

Examples:

No. 15. *Snegourotchka* 5.—Apparition of Spring. Violas + 'Cellos + Eng. horn. The same melody, *mezzo-forte cantabile* as in Ex. 9; but in a brighter key, a third higher, its resonance is more brilliant and tense. The addition of the Eng. horn makes no essential difference to the compound tone; the 'cellos stand out above the rest.

No. 16. *The Golden Cockerel* 71. Violas + 'Cellos muted.-40-

d) Violins + 'Cellos.—A combination similar to the preceding one. The 'cello tone prevails and the resonance is fuller.

Examples:

No. 17. *Snegourotchka* 288. "Spring descends upon the lake". Vns I + Vns II + 'Cellos + Eng. horn. The same *cantabile* as in Ex. 9, and 15. The Eng. horn is absorbed in the musical texture, the principal colour being that of the 'cellos. Still more powerful in resonance.

No. 18. *The May Night.* Act III L. Chorus of *Roussâlki*. The combination of the solo 'cello with the violins gives the latter a touch of the 'cello timbre.

e) Vns I + II + Violas + 'Cellos.—Combining violins, violas and 'cellos in unison is not possible except in the alto-tenor register; this process unites the full resonance of the instruments into an *ensemble* of complex quality, very tense and powerful in *forte* passages, extremely full and rich in *piano*.

Examples:

No. 19. *Shéhérazade*, 2nd movement P.—Energetic phrase *ff*.

Mlada, Lithuanian dance, before 36.

Mlada, Act III. 40.—Cleopatra's dance. *Cantabile* embellished in oriental fashion.

f) Violoncellos + D. basses.—A combination of rich full resonance, used occasionally for phrases in the very low register.

Examples:

No. 20. *Sadko* 260.—A persistent *forte* figure, severe in character.

No. 21. *Legend of Kitesh* 240.—A *pianissimo* phrase, sinister and horrible in character.

Stringed instruments doubling in octaves.

a) Vns I and Vns II in octaves.

This is a very common process used for all kinds of melodic figures, in particular those in the very high register. It has already been stated that the *E* string diminishes in fulness of tone-41- the higher it ascends from the limits of the soprano voice. Moreover, melodic figures in the very high register of the violins become too isolated from the rest of the *ensemble* unless doubled in octaves. Such doubling secures expression, fulness of tone and firmness of timbre. The reader will find numerous examples of violins in octaves; a few are added below, chiefly broad and expressive phrases.

Examples:

No. 22. *The Tsar's Bride* 166. *Cantabile, piano.*

The Tsar's Bride 206. *Cantabile, mezzo-piano*; the lower part is in unison with the soprano voice.

Shéhérazade, 3rd movement J. *Cantabile* in G major; *dolce* and *cantabile* (the same as Ex. 12).

No. 23. *The Legend of Tsar Saltan* 227. Melody with reiterated notes, *dolce, espress. e cantabile.*

Sadko, Symphonic tableau 12.

Vns I
Vns II $\rfloor 8$

muted. A short dance phrase *pianissimo*, given first to the violas, then to the violins (cf. Ex. 6).

No. 24. *Sadko*, opera 207. Perhaps an unique example of its kind; violins playing in the very extremity of the high register.

Note. This passage is difficult but nevertheless quite playable. One or two desks of the 1st Violins are sufficient to double the melody in the upper octave, all the other 1st Violins can play the octave below. In this way the piercing quality of the highest notes will be diminished, the melody will acquire a clearer and more pleasant sound, and the expressive tone quality of the lower octave will be strengthened.

**The Golden Cockerel* 156.

* " " " 165.

* *Antar*, 1st movement 11.

* No. 25. *Ivan the Terrible*, Act III 63.

b) Violins *divisi* in octaves.

First and second violins divided in two parts and progressing in octaves will deprive the melody of resonance, since the number of players is diminished by half, the consequences being specially noticeable in small orchestras. Nevertheless the method can be used occasionally when the strings are doubled by the wood-wind, and when the melody falls in a sufficiently high register.-42-

Examples:

Snegourotchka 166.—

Vns I
Vns II $]8$

mezzo-forte espressivo. Partial doubling of Coupava's song (Sopr.). One flute and one oboe double the melody.

No. 26. *Snegourotchka* 283.—Chorus of Flowers—

2 Vns soli
Vns I + Fl. I $]8.$

Pianissimo cantabile in two octaves, progressing with the women's chorus (Sopr. I), and given out earlier by the Eng. horn. The flute and all the 1st Violins except two play in the lower octave, the two solo violins, only, in the upper. The solo desk will be sufficiently prominent owing to the general *pianissimo*.

c) Violins and Violas in octaves.

First and second Violins progressing with the Violas in octaves is a common method, especially when the lower octave in the melody happens to go below the open *G* string on the violins.

1. $\left.\begin{array}{l}\text{Vns (I or II)}\\\text{Violas}\end{array}\right]8.$

Example:

Snegourotchka 137, finale of Act I. Quick melody, *piano*.

2. $\left.\begin{array}{l}\text{Vns I + II}\\\text{Violas}\end{array}\right]8$ and 3. $\left.\begin{array}{l}\text{Vns I}\\\text{Vns II + Violas}\end{array}\right]8.$

These two distributions are not exactly the same. The first should be used to obtain greater brilliance in the upper part, the second to give the lower part a fuller and more *cantabile* quality.

Examples:

No. 27. *Sadko*, before 181.—

$\left.\begin{array}{l}\text{Vns I + II}\\\text{Violas}\end{array}\right]8.$

Quick animated passage, *forte*, introducing reiterated notes.

No. 28. *Snegourotchka* 137, finale to Act I—

$\left.\begin{array}{l}\text{Vns I}\\\text{Vns II + Violas}\end{array}\right]8.$

Cantabile phrase, transmitted to the flute and clarinet (cf. Ex. 8).

d) Violas and Violoncellos in octaves.

Of special use when the Violins are otherwise employed.

Example:

* *Legend of Kitesh* 59,

$\left.\begin{array}{l}\text{Violas}\\\text{Cellos}\end{array}\right]8,$

doubled by bassoons.

e) Violins and Violoncellos in octaves.

Used in very expressive passages where the 'cellos have to play on the *A* or *D* strings. This method produces a more resonant tone than the preceding one; instances of it are frequent.-43-

Examples:

No. 29. *Antar* 43.—

Vns I + Vns II
'Cellos] 8.

Cantabile of Eastern origin.

Shéhérazade, 3rd movement H.—

Vns I
'Cellos] 8.

Cantabile mezzo-forte appassionato (cf. Ex. 1).

* No. 30. *Shéhérazade*, 3rd movement, before P—

Vns I
Vns II + 'Cellos] 8 and Vns I + II
'Cellos] 8.

The first arrangement is rarely found.

Pan Voyevoda 134, nocturne "Moonlight"—

Vns I
'Cellos] 8.

Cantabile melody given first to 'cellos alone (cf. Ex. 7).

The May Night, Act III B, C, D—

Vns I + Vns II
'Cellos] 8.

A *forte* melodic phrase.

f) Violoncellos and Double basses in octaves.

The bass is usually constructed in this manner. Examples of it are to be found everywhere. Sometimes the double bass part is simplified in comparison with the 'cello part.

Example:

Snegourotchka 9, Fairy Spring's *Aria*.

g) Violas and Double basses in octaves.

This combination seldom arises and is only used when the 'cellos are otherwise employed.

Example:

<u>No. 31.</u> *Legend of Kitesh* 223.

h) Parts progressing in octaves, each part doubled in unison. Melodies situated in the middle orchestral range may be allotted to 1st and 2nd Vns, in octaves with Violas and 'Cellos. This arrangement is constantly found, and produces a beautiful quality of tone, somewhat severe in character.

Examples:

Snegourotchka 58, 60, 65 and 68. The same melody, played twice *pianissimo*, not doubled, then twice (*mezzo-forte* and *forte*), doubled in the wood-wind.-44-

Mlada, Act II, the beginning of the Lithuanian dance. A lively *piano* theme.

Ivan the Terrible, Act II 28.

Note I. It may be of use to point out that melodies lying in the extreme upper register, e.g. those exceeding the middle of the 5th octave, are generally doubled an octave below, whilst those situated in the extreme low register (below the middle of the 1st octave) are doubled an octave higher.

Examples:

Sadko 207 (cf. <u>Ex. 24</u>).

Note II. Progression in octaves of divided strings *of the same kind* is generally to be avoided:

Violas I 'Cellos I D. basses I
Violas II, 'Cellos II, D. basses II]8,

for, in such cases the parts are played on strings which do not correspond, and unity of tone is impaired. This, however, does not apply to violins.

Note III. The following distribution is occasionally found:

Violas + 'Cellos I
D. basses + 'Cellos II]8.

Melody in double octaves.

a) Vns I   ]8   Vns I   ]8
    Vns II   Vns II
    Violas]8   or   'Cellos]8

may be used for full *cantabile* melodies extremely tense in character, and in *forte* passages for choice.

Example:

<u>No. 32.</u> *Antar* 65.—

Vns I   ]8.
Vns II
Violas + 'Cellos]8.

b) Violas   ]8   Vns I + II   ]8   Vns I + II + Violas]8
    'Cellos   or Violas +'Cellos]8   or 'Cellos
    D. basses]8   D. basses   D. basses   ]8

are employed when the low register of each instrument is brought into play, and also to suit phrases of a rough and severe character.

Examples:

Legend of Kitesh 66, opening of the 2nd Act.

<u>No. 33.</u> *Snegourotchka* 215. Tumblers' dance.-45-

Note. The lack of balance in the distribution:

Vns I + II +Violas] 8
'Cellos
D. basses] 8

is not of any great importance, for, in such cases, the partial harmonics of one octave support the tone of the other, and *vice versa*.

Doubling in three and four octaves.

The distribution

Vns I
Vns II   ] 8
Violas   ] 8
          ] 8
'Cellos   ] 8
D. basses

is very seldom found, and as a rule, only when supported by wind instruments.

Examples:

The Legend of Kitesh 150 (*allargando*).

* *Shéhérazade*, 4th movement, commencing at the 10th bar.

Vns I
Vns II   ]
Violas + 'Cellos   ] 8.
D. basses   ]

Melody in thirds and sixths.

In confiding a melody in thirds to the strings it is frequently necessary to use the same quality of tone in both parts, but in the case of a melody in sixths different timbres may be employed. In writing thirds doubled in octaves, the first and second violins should be used. In spite of the difference in the quantity of players, the thirds will not sound unequal. The same arrangement may obtain in the viola and 'cello groups, but it is useless in the case of melody in sixths.

Examples:

* No. 34. *Legend of Kitesh* 34—

Vns I *div.*) 3
Vns II *div.*) 3] 8.

* *Legend of Kitesh* 39—

Vns I
Violas] 6.

Cf. also *Legend of Kitesh* 223:

Vns I } 3
Vns II } 3
Vns I } 3   ] 8 (Ex. 31).
Vns II } 3

Distribution in octaves, thirds, and sixths is usually regulated by the normal register of the respective instruments, so as to avoid -46- any suggestion of mannerism resulting from the disturbance of balance. But such a departure from the recognised order may be permitted in special cases. For instance, in the following example of writing in sixths the upper part is allotted to the 'cellos, the lower part to the violins on the *G* string; this arrangement produces a quality of tone distinctly original in character.

Example:

No. 35. *Spanish Capriccio* D—

'Cellos
Vns I + II] 6.

Melody in the wood-wind.

* The choice of instruments for characteristic and expressive melody is based on their distinctive qualities, discussed minutely in the foregoing chapter. To a large extent the question is left to the orchestrator's own personal taste. Only the best methods of using the wood-wind in unison or octaves, and distributing a melody in thirds, sixths and mixed intervals, from the standpoint of resonance and tone quality will be indicated in this section of the work. Examples of the use of solo wood-wind are to be found in any score; the following are typical instances:

Examples of solo wood-wind:

1. *Piccolo: Serbian Fantasia* C; No. 36. *Tsar Saltan* 216; *Snegourotchka* 54.

2. *Flute: Antar* 4; *Servilia* 80; *Snegourotchka* 79, 183; *A Fairy Tale* L; *The Christmas Night* 163; No. 37. *Shéhérazade*, 4th movement, before A (*Fl. à 2* in the low register).

Flute (double tonguing): *Pan Voyevoda* 72; *Shéhérazade*, 4th movement, after V; No. 38. *Ivan the Terrible*, Act III, after 10.

3. *Bass flute*: No. 39. *Legend of Kitesh* 44.

4. *Oboe*: No. 40. *Shéhérazade*, 2nd movement A; *The May Night*, Act III Kk; No. 41. *Snegourotchka* 50; *Snegourotchka* 112, 239; *The Tsar's Bride* 108 (cf. Ex. 284), No. 42 and 43. *The Golden Cockerel* 57 and 97.

5. *Eng. horn*: *Snegourotchka* 97, 283 (cf. Ex. 26); No. 44. *Spanish Capriccio* E; No. 45. *The Golden Cockerel* 61.-47-

6. *Small Clarinet*: No. 46. *Mlada*, Act II 33; *Mlada*, Act III 37.

7. *Clarinet*: *Serbian Fantasia* G; *Spanish Capriccio* A; *Snegourotchka* 90, 99, 224, 227, 231 (cf. Ex. 8); *The May Night*, Act I, before X; *Shéhérazade*, 3rd movement D; *A Fairy Tale* M; *The Tsar's Bride* 50, 203; *The Golden Cockerel* 97 (lowest register, cf. Ex. 43).

8. *Bass clarinet*: No. 47 and 48. *Snegourotchka* 243 and 246-247.

9. *Bassoon*: *Antar* 59; No. 49. *Vera Scheloga* 36; *Shéhérazade*, 2nd movement, beginning (cf. Ex. 40); No. 50. *The Golden Cockerel* 249; No. 51. *Mlada*, Act III, after 29; cf. also Ex. 78.

10. *Double bassoon*: *Legend of Kitesh*, before 84, 289; cf. also Ex. 10 (D. bassoon + D. bass solo).

The normal order of wood-wind instruments and that which produces the most natural resonance is the following: *Flutes, Oboes, Clarinets, Bassoons* (the order used in orchestral full scores). Departure from this natural order, e.g. placing bassoons above clarinets and oboes, or flutes below oboes and clarinets, and especially below the bassoons, creates a far-fetched, unnatural tone, useful, however, in certain cases to attain certain special effects. I do not advise the student to make too free a use of this proceeding.

Combination in unison.

The combination of two different wood-wind instruments in unison yields the following tone qualities:

a) *Flute + Oboe.* A quality fuller than that of the flute, sweeter than that of the oboe. Played softly, the flute will predominate in the low, the oboe in the upper register. Example: No. 52. *Snegourotchka* 113.

b) *Flute + Clarinet.* A quality fuller than that of the flute, duller than that of the clarinet. The flute will predominate in the lower, the clarinet in the higher register. Examples: No. 53. *Legend of Kitesh* 330; also 339 and 342.

c) *Oboe + Clarinet.* A fuller quality than that of either instrument heard separately. The dark, nasal tone of the oboe will prevail in the low register, the bright, "chest" quality of the clarinet in the high compass. Examples: *Snegourotchka* 19; No. 54. *Snegourotchka*-48- 115. Cf. also *Legend of Kitesh* 68, 70, 84—2 Ob. + 3 Cl. (Ex. 199-201).

d) *Flute + Oboe + Clarinet.* Very full in quality. The flute predominates in the low register, the oboe in the middle, and the clarinet in the high compass. Examples: *Mlada*, Act I 1; * *Sadko* 58 (2 Fl. + 2 Ob. + Small Cl.).

e) *Bassoon + Clarinet.* Very full quality. The gloomy character of the clarinet prevails in the lower register, the sickly quality of the bassoon in the higher. Example: *Mlada*, Act II, after 49.

f) *Bassoon + Oboe*, and

g) *Bassoon + Flute.*

The combinations *f* and *g*, as well as *Bassoon + Clarinet + Oboe*, and *Bassoon + Clarinet + Flute* are very seldom found except in certain orchestral *tutti*, where they produce increased resonance without creating a fresh atmosphere. But in such combinations, the range of which is practically restricted to the limits of the third octave, the low notes of the flute will predominate in the lower third of this register, and the high notes of the bassoon in the middle third. The clarinet, weak in the middle compass will not stand out prominently in this particular combination.

h) *Bassoon + Clarinet + Oboe + Flute.* This combination is equally rare. The colour is rich, and difficult to define in words. The tone of each instrument will be separated from the others more or less in the manner detailed above. Examples: *Russian Easter Fête*, the beginning; No. 55. *Snegourotchka* 301; *The May Night*, Act III Qqq.

The process of combining two or more qualities of tone in unison, while endowing the music with greater resonance, sweetness and power, possesses the disadvantage of restricting the variety of colour and expression. Individual timbres lose their characteristics when associated with others. Hence such combinations should be handled with extreme care. Phrases or melodies demanding diversity of expression alone should be entrusted to solo instruments of simple timbres. The same applies to the coupling of two instruments of the same kind, such as 2 flutes, 2 oboes, 2 clarinets, 2 bassoons. The quality of tone will lose nothing of its individuality, and will gain in power, but its capacity for expression will be diminished accordingly. An-49- instrument enjoys greater independence and freedom when used as a solo than when it is doubled. The use of doubling and mixed timbres is naturally more frequent in loud passages than in soft ones, also where expression and colour is broad rather than individual or intimate in character.

I cannot refrain from mentioning how greatly I dislike the method of duplicating all the wood-wind, in order to balance a group of strings, reinforced out of all reason, to suit the ever-growing dimensions of concert halls. I am convinced that, artistically speaking, a limit should be set to the size of both concert room and orchestra. The music performed at these super-concerts must be specially composed on a plan of its own—a subject which cannot be considered here.

Combination in octaves.

When the melody is entrusted to two wood-wind instruments in octaves, the usual arrangement producing natural resonance is:

$$8\begin{bmatrix} \text{Fl.} & \text{Fl.} & \text{Fl.} & \text{Ob.} & \text{Ob.} & \text{Cl.} \\ \text{Ob.} & \text{Cl.} & \text{Fag.} & \text{Cl.} & \text{Fag.} & \text{Fag.} \end{bmatrix}8$$

The combination of flute and bassoon in octaves is rare on account of the widely separated registers of the two instruments. Deviation from the natural order, such as placing the bassoon above the clarinet or oboe, the clarinet above the oboe or flute etc., creates an unnatural resonance occasioned by the confusion of registers, the instrument of lower compass playing in its high register and *vice versa*. The lack of proper relationship between the different tone qualities then becomes apparent.

Examples:

<u>No. 56.</u> *Spanish Capriccio* O—

$\begin{matrix} \text{Fl.} \\ \text{Ob.} \end{matrix}]8.$

<u>No. 57.</u> *Snegourotchka* 254—

$\begin{matrix} \text{Fl.} \\ \text{Eng. horn} \end{matrix}]8.$

* <u>No. 58.</u> *Shéhérazade*, 3rd movement E—

$\begin{matrix} \text{Fl.} \\ \text{Cl.} \end{matrix}]8.$

Sadko 195—

$\begin{matrix} \text{Fl.} \\ \text{Eng. horn} \end{matrix}]8.$

Pan Voyevoda 132—

Fl.
Cl.] 8.

Tsar Saltan 39—

Cl.
Fag.] 8.

<u>No. 59.</u> *Vera Scheloga* 30—

Cl.
Fag.] 8,

likewise any number of examples in the scores of various composers.

The use of two instruments of the same colour in octaves, e.g. 2 flutes, 2 clarinets or 2 bassoons etc., if not exactly to be avoided -50- is certainly not to be recommended, as the instruments, playing in different registers will not correspond one with the other. Nevertheless this method may be safely employed when stringed instruments, *arco* or *pizzicato* double the two members of the wood-wind, and especially in the middle compass. The process is most satisfactory for repeated notes or sustained passages.

Examples:

The May Night, Act I T—

Cl. I
Cl. II] 8.

* *Sadko*, after 159—

Ob. I
Ob. II] 3, doubled by *pizz.* strings.

* *Servilia*, after 21—

Fag. I
Fag. II] 8 + *pizz.* strings.

Instruments of the same branch playing in octaves, e.g.

8 [Fag.　　Cl.　　　Ob.　　　Small cl.　Flute　　Picc.　　] 8
　　C-Fag.　Cl. basso　Eng. horn　Clar.　　　Alto Fl.　Fl.

always produce a good effect.

Examples:

Snegourotchka 5—

Picc.
Fl.] 8 (cf. Ex. 15).

The Tsar's Bride 133—

Picc.
Fl.] 8.

Tsar Saltan 216—

Picc.
Fl.] 8 (cf. Ex. 36).

Sadko, after 59

Small cl.
Cl.] 8.

Legend of Kitesh 240—

Fag.
C-Fag.] 8 (cf. Ex. 21).

<u>No 60.</u> *Mlada*, Act III, before 44—

Ob.
Eng. horn] 8.

As in the strings, so in the wood-wind it is advisable to double in octaves any melody situated in the extremely high or low compass; an octave lower in the first case, an octave higher in the second. Thus the piccolo will be doubled by the flute, oboe or clarinet an octave lower; the double bassoon will be doubled by bassoon, clarinet or bass clarinet an octave higher.

8 [Picc. Picc. Picc.
     Fl.   Ob.   Cl.] 8

$$8\begin{bmatrix}\text{Fag.} & \text{Bass cl.} & \text{Cl.} & \text{Cl.} & \text{Fag.} & \text{Fag.} \\ \text{C-Fag.} & \text{Fag.} & \text{Fag.} & \text{Bass cl.} & \text{Fag.} & \text{Bass cl.}\end{bmatrix}8$$

Examples:

* *Tsar Saltan* 39—

$$\left.\begin{array}{l}\text{Picc.}\\ \text{Ob.}\end{array}\right]8.$$

* <u>No. 61.</u> *Mlada*, Act II, Lithuanian dance 32—

$$\left.\begin{array}{l}\text{Picc.}\\ \text{Small cl.}\end{array}\right]8.$$

-51-

Sadko 150—

$$\left.\begin{array}{l}\text{Picc.}\\ \text{Small cl.}\end{array}\right]8.$$

* Mixed qualities of tone may be employed in doubling in octaves, the above remarks still holding good.

Examples:

Pan Voyevoda 134—

$$\left.\begin{array}{l}\text{Cl. + Ob.}\\ \text{Cl. + Eng. horn}\end{array}\right]8\ (\text{cf. }\underline{\text{Ex. 7}}).$$

<u>No. 62.</u> *Servilia* 168—

$$\left.\begin{array}{l}\text{2 Fl. + Ob.}\\ \text{2 Cl. + Eng. horn}\end{array}\right]8.$$

<u>No. 63.</u> *The Tsar's Bride* 120—

$$\left.\begin{array}{l}\text{3 Fl. + Ob.}\\ \text{2 Cl. + Fag. + Eng. horn}\end{array}\right]8.$$

Mlada, Act III 41—

Fl. + Bass fl.
Cl. + Bass cl.] 8.

Doubling in two, three and four octaves.

In such cases the student should follow the above-mentioned rules, and should take care not to infringe the natural order:

In 3 octaves:
Fl. Ob. Fl. Fl.
Ob. Cl. Cl. Ob.] 8
Cl. Fag. Fag. Fag.] 8.

In 4 octaves:
Fl.
Ob.] 8
Cl.] 8
Fag.] 8.

Mixed timbres may also be employed.

Examples:

<u>No. 64.</u> *Spanish Capriccio* P—melody in 4 octaves:

Picc.
2 Fl.] 8
2 Ob. + Cl.] 8
Fag.] 8.

The Tsar's Bride 141—melody in 3 octaves.

* *Legend of Kitesh* 212—

2 Cl.
Bass cl.] 8
D. bassoon] 8.

* <u>No. 65.</u> *Antar*, (1st version) 3rd movement, the beginning—

Picc. + 2 Fl.
2 Ob. + 2 Cl.] 8
2 Fag.] 8;

also C, melody in 4 octaves (piccolo in the upper octaves).

* *Mlada*, Act III, after 42—

Fl.
Ob.   ] 8
Eng. horn] 8.

<u>No. 66.</u> *Shéhérazade*, 3rd movement G—

Picc.
Cl. I   ] 8
Cl. II   ] 8.

Examples of melody doubled in five octaves are extremely rare; in such cases the strings participate in the process.-52-

Melody in thirds and sixths.

Melodic progression in thirds and sixths demands either two instruments of the same colour (2 Fl., 2 Ob., 2 Cl., 2 Fag.), or instruments of different colours in the normal order of register:

Fl. Fl. Ob. Cl. Ob.
Ob. Cl. Cl. Fag. Fag.] 3 (6).

If this order is inverted, e.g.

Ob. Cl. Fag.
Fl. Fl. Cl.] 3 (6),

a strained and forced resonance is created. For progressions in thirds, the best method, from the standpoint of equality in tone is to use instruments of the same kind in pairs; for progressions in sixths instruments of different kinds are more suitable, but both courses are good and useful. They may also be employed for progressions in thirds and sixths, or thirds, fifths and sixths mixed, as for example:

[Listen]

Examples:

Legend of Kitesh 24—different wind instruments in turn.

The May Night, Act III G—

$\left.\begin{array}{l}\text{Cl.}\\\text{Cl.}\end{array}\right]3.$

Sadko 279-280—

$\left.\begin{array}{l}\text{Fl.}\\\text{Fl.}\end{array}\right]3\ (6).$

<u>No. 67.</u> *Spanish Capriccio*, before V—various wood-wind in thirds and sixths.

Servilia 228—

$\left.\begin{array}{l}\text{Fl.}\\\text{Fl.}\end{array}\right]3$ and $\left.\begin{array}{l}\text{Cl.}\\\text{Cl.}\end{array}\right]3.$

The Golden Cockerel 232—

$\left.\begin{array}{l}\text{2 Fl.}\\\text{2 Ob.}\end{array}\right]6.$

* *Sadko* 43—All wood-wind in turn, simple timbres.

When the doubled parts progress in thirds or sixths, the following method is advisable:

$\left.\begin{array}{l}\text{Fl. + Ob.}\\\text{Fl. + Ob.}\end{array}\right]3\ (6)$ or $\left.\begin{array}{l}\text{Fl. + Cl.}\\\text{Fl. + Cl.}\end{array}\right]3\ (6)$ etc., as well as:

$\left.\begin{array}{l}\text{Fl. + Ob.}\\\text{Fl. + Cl.}\end{array}\right]3\ (6)$ or $\left.\begin{array}{l}\text{Ob. + Fl.}\\\text{Fl. + Cl.}\end{array}\right]3\ (6)$ etc.

In the case of tripling the following arrangement may be adopted:

$\left.\begin{array}{l}\text{Fl. + Ob. + Cl.}\\\text{Fl. + Ob. + Cl.}\end{array}\right]3\ (6)$ or $\left.\begin{array}{l}\text{Ob. + 2 Fl.}\\\text{Ob. + 2 Cl.}\end{array}\right]3\ (6)$ etc.

Examples:

* <u>No. 68.</u> *The Christmas Night* 187—

Ob. + Cl.
Ob. + Cl. } 3.

* *Legend of Kitesh* 202-203 different mixed timbres.-53-

Thirds and sixths together.

[Listen]

Apart from the obvious distribution:

Fl.   Ob.
Ob. or Cl.
Cl.   Fag.,

there are certain complicated methods which involve doubling:

Upper part. Ob. + Fl.
Middle "   Fl. + Cl.
Lower "   Ob. + Cl.

The following is a complex instance somewhat vague in character:

<u>No. 69.</u> Legend of Kitesh 35—

Ob.   Fl.
Ob. + Cl. and Fl. + Ob.
Cl.   Ob.

Melody in the brass.

The natural scale, the only one which brass instruments had at their disposal prior to the invention of valves was:

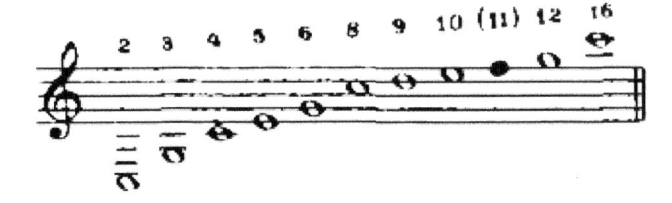

[Listen]

giving, in two part harmony:

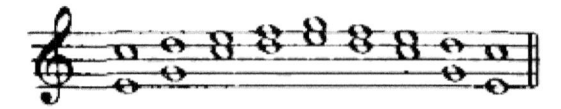

[Listen]

With the help of rhythm, these component parts have given rise to a whole series of themes and phrases named fanfares, trumpet calls or flourishes, best adapted to the character of brass instruments.

In modern music, thanks to the introduction of valves, this scale is now possible in all keys for every chromatic brass instrument, without it being necessary to change the key, and the addition of a few notes foreign to the natural scale has enriched the possibilities of these flourishes and fanfares, and endowed them with greater variety of expression.

These phrases, either as solos, or in two or three parts, fall specially to the lot of the trumpets and horns, but they may also be given to the trombones. The full, clear, ringing notes of the middle and upper register of horns and trumpets are best suited to figures of this description.-54-

Examples:

Servilia 20—Trumpets.

The Christmas Night 182—Horn, Trumpets.

Vera Scheloga, beginning of Overture, and after 45—Horn, Trumpets.

Ivan the Terrible, Act III 3—Cornet.

Snegourotchka 155—Trumpets.

No. 70. *Legend of Kitesh* 65 and elsewhere.—3 Trumpets, 4 Horns.

Pan Voyevoda 191—2 Trombones, Trumpet.

* *The Golden Cockerel* 20—2 Horns and

Trumpets
Horns] 8 (cf. further on).

After fanfare figures, those melodies best suited to the brass quality are those of an unmodulated diatonic character, rousing and triumphant in the major key, dark and gloomy in the minor.

Examples:

No. 71. *Sadko* 342—Trumpet.

Sadko, before 181—Trombones (cf. Ex. 27).

No. 72. *Snegourotchka* 71—Trumpet.

Russian Easter Fête M—Trombone.

Spanish Capriccio E—Alternative use in the horn of open and stopped notes (cf. Ex. 44).

Ivan the Terrible, Act II, before 17—Bass trumpet, and 3 Horns a little further on.

Mlada, Act II 33—Bass trumpet (cf. Ex. 46).

The genial and poetic tone of the horn in *piano* passages affords greater scope in the choice of melodies and phrases that may be entrusted to this instrument.

Examples:

The May Night, Overture 13.

The Christmas Night 1.

Snegourotchka 86.

Pan Voyevoda 37.

No. 73. *Antar* 40.-55-

Melodies involving chromatic or enharmonic writing are much less suitable to the character of brass instruments. Nevertheless such melodies may sometimes be allotted to the brass, as in the music of Wagner, and the modern Italian realists, who, however, carry the proceeding to extremes. Vigourous phrases in the form of a fanfare, although introducing chromatic notes sound singularly beautiful on the brass.

Example:

No. 74. *Shéhérazade*, 2nd movement D.

As a general rule, brass instruments lack the capacity to express passion or geniality. Phrases charged with these sentiments become sickly and insipid when confided to the brass. Energetic power, free or restrained, simplicity and eloquence constitute the valuable qualities of this group.

Brass in unison, in octaves, thirds and sixths.

As, from its very nature, the brass is not called upon to realise a wide range of expression, kindred instruments of one group may be employed *solo*, as well as in unison. The combination of 3 trombones or 4 horns in unison is frequently met with, and produces extreme power and resonance of tone.

Examples:

Snegourotchka 5—4 Horns (cf. Ex. 15).

Snegourotchka 199—4 Horns and 2 Trumpets.

Sadko 175—1, 2, 3 Trumpets.

No. 75. *Sadko* 305[13]—3 Trombones.

No. 76. *The May Night*, beginning of Act III—1, 2, 3, 4 Horns.

Legend of Kitesh, end of Act I—4 Horns (cf. Ex. 70).

No. 77. *Shéhérazade*, 4th movement p. 204—3 Trombones.

Mlada; Lithuanian dance—6 Horns (cf. Ex. 61).-56-

Owing to the resonant power of the entire group, the equality and even gradation of tone between the dark colour of the deep compass and the bright quality of the upper register, the use of brass instruments of the same kind in octaves, thirds or sixths invariably leads to satisfactory results. For the same reason the employment of brass instruments of different kinds, arranged according to normal order of register:

Trumpet	Trumpet	Trombone	2 Trombones	2 Trumpets	2 Horns
2 Horns	Trombone	Tuba	Trombone + Tuba	2 Trombones	Tuba

is likewise successful whether the instruments are doubled or not. Another possible method, though not so reliable, is to combine horns (above) with trombones, exclusively in octaves:

2 Horns / 1 Trombone] 8 or 4 Horns / 2 Trombones] 8.

Examples:

Sadko, before 120—

Trumpet / Trumpet] 8.

Sadko 5—

2 Trumpets / 4 Horns] 8.

Snegourotchka 222—

2 Trombones / Trombone + Tuba] 8.

Ivan the Terrible, Act III 10

1 Trombone + Trumpet / 2 Trombones] 8 (cf. Ex. 38).

The Golden Cockerel 125—

Trumpet / Trombone] 8.

Cf. also *Snegourotchka* 325-326—

Trombone / Trombone] 8 (Ex. 95).

Melody in different groups of instruments combined together.

A. Combination of wind and brass in unison.

The combination of a wood-wind and brass instrument produces a complex resonance in which the tone of the brass predominates. This resonance is naturally more powerful than that of each instrument taken separately, but slightly sweeter than the brass instrument alone. The tone of the wood-wind blends with that of the brass, softens and rarefies it, as in the process of combining two wood-wind instruments of different colour. Instances of such doubling are fairly numerous, especially in *forte* passages. The trumpet is the instrument most frequently doubled: Trumpet + Cl., Trumpet + Ob., Trumpet + Fl., as well as Trumpet + Cl. + Ob. + Fl.;-57- the horn, less often: Horn + Cl., Horn + Fag. Trombones and Tuba may also be doubled: Trombone + Fag., Tuba + Fag. Combining the Eng. horn, bass clarinet and double bassoon with the brass, in corresponding registers, presents the same characteristics.

Examples:

Legend of Kitesh 56—Trombone + Eng. horn.

* *Mlada*, Act III, before 34—3 Trombones + Bass cl.

As a rule, the addition of a wind to a brass instrument yields a finer legato effect than when the latter instrument plays alone.

B. Combination of wind and brass in octaves.

Doubling the horns in octaves by clarinets, oboes or flutes often replaces the combination

1 Trumpet
1 Horn (or 2 Horns)] 8.

This is done when it is a question of introducing a rich tone into the upper octave which the trumpet is not capable of imparting. If a single horn is used, the upper part is allotted to 2 clarinets, 2 oboes, or 2 flutes. But if there are two horns playing the lower octave in unison, three or four wind instruments will be necessary above, especially in *forte* passages:

8 [2 Ob. or 2 Cl. or 2 Fl.
    1 Horn   as well as 2 Ob. + 1 Cl.
                                        1 Horn   ] 8; 2 Fl. + 2 Cl.
                                                            2 Horns   ] 8.

To double a trumpet in the upper octave three or four wind instruments are required, but in the top register two flutes will suffice.

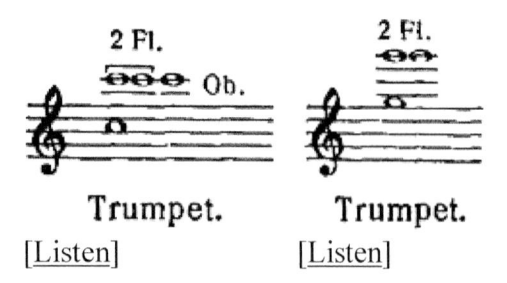

[Listen]   [Listen]

Wood-wind instruments should not be used to double a trombone in the octave above; trumpets are more suitable.

Examples of doubling in octaves:

* *Snegourotchka* 71—

Ob. + Cl.
Horn] 8.

* *Legend of Tsar Saltan*, before 180—

Ob. + Cl.] 6
Ob. + Cl.   ] 8.
Horn   ] 6
Horn

-58-

* Mention should also be made of mixed timbres (wood and brass) in progression in octaves.

Examples:

Mlada, Act III, beginning of Scene III—

Trombone + Bass cl.
Tuba + C-fag.] 8.

No. 78. *Mlada*, Act III after 25—

2 Cl. + 2 Horns + Trombone
Bass cl. + 2 Horns + Trombone] 8 (low register).

No. 79. *Mlada*, Act III, before 35—general unison.

When it is desired to distribute the melody over three or four octaves, it is difficult to achieve perfect balance of tone.

Examples:

* *Shéhérazade*, 4th movement, 15th bar after W—

Picc.
2 Fl. + 2 Ob.] 8
2 Trumpets   ] 8.

* *Legend of Tsar Saltan* 228—

Picc.
2 Fl. + 2 Ob.   ] 8
Trumpet + Eng. horn   ] 8.

C. Combination of strings and wind.

In commencing this section of the work I consider it necessary to lay down the following fundamental rules which apply equally to melody, harmony, counterpoint and polyphonic writing.

All combinations of strings and wood-wind are good; a wind instrument progressing in unison with a stringed instrument increases the resonance of the latter and amplifies its tone, while the quality of the strings softens that of the wood-wind. In such combinations the strings will predominate provided that the two instruments are of equal power, e.g. when violins are coupled with an oboe, a bassoon with the 'cellos. If several wind instruments play in unison with one group of strings, the latter will be overpowered. As a rule all combinations refine the characteristics of each instrument taken separately, the wood-wind losing more than the strings.

Doubling in unison.

The best and most natural combinations are between instruments whose registers correspond the nearest:

Vns + Fl. (Bass fl., picc.), Vns + Ob., Vns + Cl. (small Cl.);

Violas + Ob. (Eng. horn), Violas + Cl., Violas + Fag.

'Cellos + Cl. (Bass cl.), 'Cellos + Fag.;-59-

D. basses + Bass cl., D. basses + Fag.; D. basses + C-fag.

The object of these combinations is: a) to obtain a new timbre of definite colour; b) to strengthen the resonance of the strings; c) to soften the quality of the wood-wind.

Examples:

Snegourotchka 5—'Cellos + Violas + Eng. horn (cf. Ex. 15).

" 28—Violas + Ob. + Eng. horn.

" 116—Vns I + II + Ob. + Cl.

" 288—Vns I + II + 'Cellos + Eng. horn (cf. Ex. 17).

No. 80. *The May Night*, Act III Bb—Violas + Cl.

No. 81. *Sadko* 311—Vns + Ob.

No. 82. " 77—Violas + Eng. horn.

No. 83. " 123—Violas + Eng. horn.

Servilia 59—Vns G string + Fl.

Tsar Saltan 30—Vns I + II + 2 Cl.

No. 84. *Tsar Saltan* 30, 10th bar.—'Cellos + Violas + 3 Cl. + Fag.

Tsar Saltan 156-159—Vns detached + Fl. *legato*.

The Tsar's Bride 10 Violas + 'Cellos + Fag.

Antar, 4th movement 63—'Cellos + 2 Fag.

Shéhérazade, 3rd movement H—Violas + Ob. + Eng. horn.

Parts doubled in octaves.

Examples of strings in octaves doubled by wood-wind also in octaves are numerous, and do not require special description; they are used according to the rules already laid down. The following are examples of melody distributed over 1, 2, 3 and 4 octaves:

Examples:

No. 85. *Ivan the Terrible*, beginning of Overture—

Vns I + II + 2 Cl.
Violas + 'Cellos + 2 Fag.] 8.

No. 86. *Sadko* 3—

'Cellos + Bass cl.
D. basses + C-fag.] 8.

Sadko 166—

'Cellos + Fag.
D. basses + C-fag.] 8.

" 235—

Violas + 2 Cl.
'Cellos + D. basses + 2 Fag.] 8.

The Tsar's Bride 14—

'Cellos + Fag.
D. basses + Fag.] 8.

-60-

" " " 81—

Vns I div. + Fl.
Vns II + Ob.] 8.

" " " 166—

Vns I + Fl.
Vns II + Ob.] 8 (cf. Ex. 22).

In three and four octaves:

Servilia 93—

Vns + 3 Fl.
Violas + 2 Ob.] 8
'Cellos + 2 Fag.] 8.

No. 87. *Kashtcheï* 105—

Vns I + Picc.
Vns II + Fl. + Ob.] 8
Violas + 'Cellos + 2 Cl. + Eng. horn + Fag.] 8.

Shéhérazade, 3rd movement M—

Vns I + Fl.
Vns II + Ob.] 8
'Cellos + Engl. horn] 8.

Examples of melody in thirds and sixths:

Servilia 44—

Fl. + Ob. + Cl. + Vns
Fl. + Ob. + Cl. + Vns div.] 3.

No. 88. *Servilia* 111—Strings and wood-wind in thirds.

No. 89. " 125—same combination, in thirds and sixths.

Kashtcheï 90—The same.

It is necessary to pay more attention to cases where, of the two parts in octaves, only one is doubled. When this method is applied to a melody in the soprano register it is better to allow the wood-wind to progress in octaves, the lower part only being doubled by one of the string groups;

Picc.   Fl.
Fl. + Vns] 8.   Ob. (Cl.) + Vns] 8.

Examples:

Tsar Saltan 102—

2 Fl. + Picc.
Vns I + II + Ob.] 8 (cf. Ex. 133).

* No. 90. *Shéhérazade*, 4th movement U—

2 Cl.
'Cellos + 2 Horns] 8.

In the case of a melody in the low register demanding a sweet soft tone, the violoncellos and double basses should be made to progress in octaves, the former doubled by a bassoon, the latter not doubled at all:

'Cellos + Fag.
D. basses] 8.

Sometimes a composer is obliged to use this method on account of the very low register of the double bass, especially if a double bassoon is not included in his orchestral scheme.[14]

-61-

Example:

No. 91. *Tsar Saltan* 92—

Violas + Fag.
'Cellos + Fag.] 8
D. basses] 8.

D. Combination of strings and brass.

Owing to the dissimilarity between the quality of string and brass tone, the combination of these two groups in unison can never yield such a perfect blend as that produced by the union of strings and wood-wind. When a brass and a stringed instrument progress in unison, each can be heard separately, but the instruments in each group which can be combined with the greatest amount of success are those whose respective registers correspond the most nearly; Violin + Trumpet; Viola + Horn;

'Cellos   Trombones
          +
D. basses   Tuba

(for heavy massive effects).

The combination of horns and 'cellos, frequently employed, produces a beautifully blended, soft quality of tone.

Examples:

Tsar Saltan 29—Vns I + II + Horn.

* No. 92. *The Golden Cockerel* 98—Violas *con sord.* + Horn.

E. Combination of the three groups.

The combination of members of the three groups in unison is more common, the presence of the wood-wind imparting a fuller and more evenly blended tone. The question as to which group will predominate in timbre depends upon the number of instruments employed. The most natural combinations, and those most generally in use are:

Vns + Ob. (Fr., Cl.) + Trumpet;
Violas (or 'Cellos) + Cl. (Eng. horn) + Horn;
'Cellos
         + 2 Fag. + 3 Trombones + Tuba.
D. basses

Such groupings are used for preference in loud passages or for a heavy *piano* effect.

Examples:

No. 93-94. *Snegourotchka* 218 and 219—Vns I + II + Cl. + -62-Horn and Vns I + II + Cl. + Trumpet.

Servilia 168—

Violas + Trombones
'Cellos + Trombone + Bass Cl. $\left.\begin{array}{l}\ \\ \ \end{array}\right] \begin{array}{l} 8 \\ 8 \end{array}$ (cf. Ex. 62).
D. basses + Tuba + Fag.

No. 95. *Snegourotchka* 325—

'Cellos + Violas + Fag. + Trombone
D. basses + Fag. + Tuba $\left.\begin{array}{l}\ \\ \ \end{array}\right] 8.$

Pan Voyevoda 224—Vns + Fag. + Horn + Vn. + Cl. + Trumpet. (Stopped notes in the brass.)

* *Mlada*, Act III, after 23—Violas + 2 Cl. + Bass trumpet.

* No. 96. *Ivan the Terrible*, Act III, before 66—

Bass Cl. + Horn
D. basses + C-fag. + Tuba $\left.\begin{array}{l}\ \\ \ \end{array}\right] 8.$

* *Ivan the Terrible*, Overture, 4th bar after 9—Violas + 'Cellos + Eng. horn + 2 Cl. + Bass Cl. + 2 Fag. + 4 Horns. (The melody simplified in the horns.)

Chapter III.

HARMONY.

General observations.

The art of orchestration demands a beautiful and well-balanced distribution of chords forming the harmonic texture. Moreover, transparence, accuracy and purity in the movement of each part are essential conditions if satisfactory resonance is to be obtained. No perfection in resonance can accrue from faulty progression of parts.

Note. There are people who consider orchestration simply as the art of selecting instruments and tone qualities, believing that if an orchestral score does not sound well, it is entirely due to the choice of instruments and timbres. But unsatisfactory resonance is often solely the outcome of faulty handling of parts, and such a composition will continue to sound badly whatever choice of instruments is made. So, on the other hand, it often happens that a passage in which the chords are properly distributed, and the progression of parts correctly handled, will sound equally well if played by strings, wood-wind or brass.

The composer should picture to himself the exact harmonic formation of the piece he intends to orchestrate. If, in his rough sketch, there exist any uncertainly as to the number or movement of harmonic parts, he is advised to settle this at once. It is likewise essential for him to form a clear idea as to the construction and musical elements of the piece, and to realise the exact nature and limitations of the themes, phrases and ideas he is going to employ. Every transition from one order of harmonic writing to another, from four-part harmony to three, or from five-part harmony to unison etc., must coincide with the introduction of a new idea, a fresh theme or phrase; otherwise the orchestrator will encounter many unforeseen and insurmountable difficul-64-ties. For example, if, during a passage written in four parts a chord in five-part harmony is introduced, a fresh instrument must needs be added to play this particular fifth part, and this addition may easily damage the resonance of the chord in question, and render the resolution of a discord or the correct progression of parts impossible.

Number of harmonic parts—Duplication.

In the very large majority of cases harmony is written in four parts; this applies not only to single chords or a succession of them, but also to the formation of the harmonic basis. Harmony which at first sight appears to comprise 5, 6, 7 and 8 parts, is usually only four part harmony with extra parts added. These additions are nothing more than the duplication in the adjacent upper octave of one or more of the three upper parts forming the original harmony, the bass being doubled in the lower octave only. The following diagrams will explain my meaning:

A. Close part-writing.

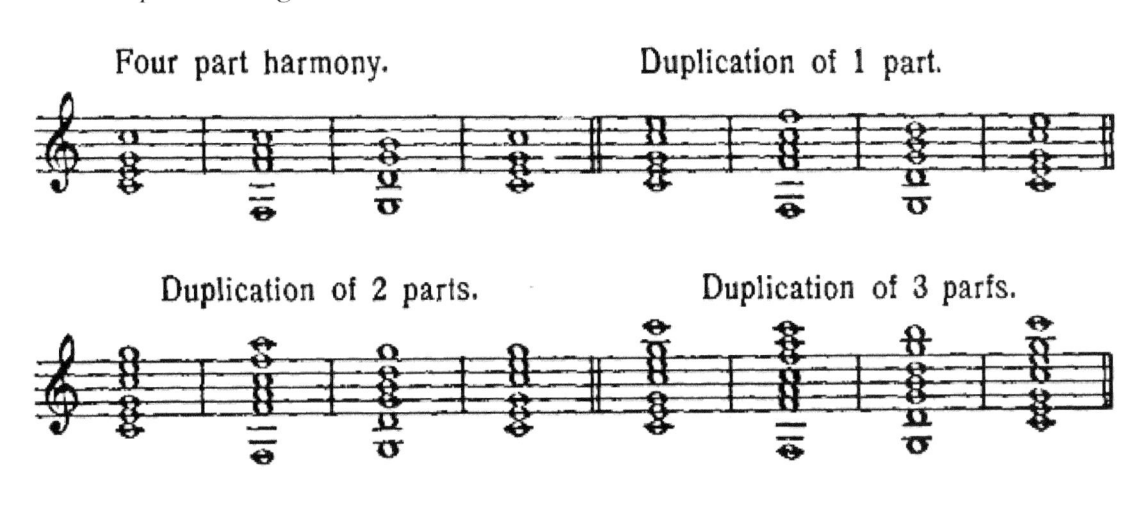

[Listen]

B. Widely-divided part-writing.

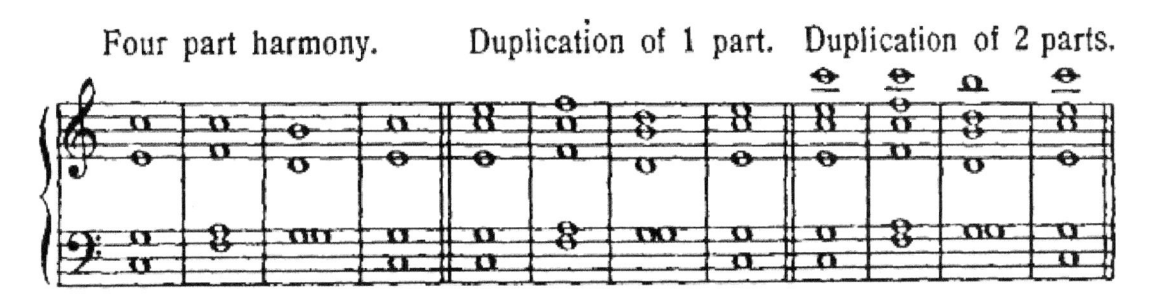

[Listen]

Note. In widely-spaced harmony only the soprano and alto parts may be doubled in octaves. Duplicating the tenor part is to be avoided, as close writing is thereby produced, and doubling the bass part creates an effect of heaviness. The bass part should never mix with the others:-65-

Bad:

[Listen]

On account of the distance between the bass and the three other parts, only partial duplication is possible.

Good:

[Listen]

Note. Notes in unison resulting from correct duplication need not be avoided, for although the tone in such cases is not absolutely uniform, the ear will be satisfied with the correct progression of parts.

Consecutive octaves between the upper parts are not permissible:

Bad:

[Listen]

Consecutive fifths resulting from the duplication of the three upper parts moving in chords of sixths are of no importance:

Good:

[Listen]

The bass of an inversion of the dominant chord should never be doubled in any of the upper parts:

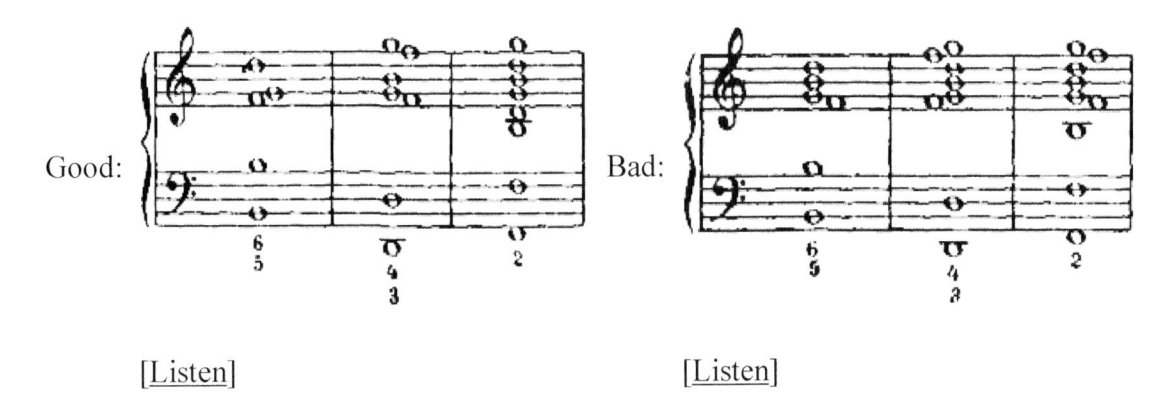

Good: Bad:

[Listen]   [Listen]

This applies also to other chords of the seventh and diminished seventh:-66-

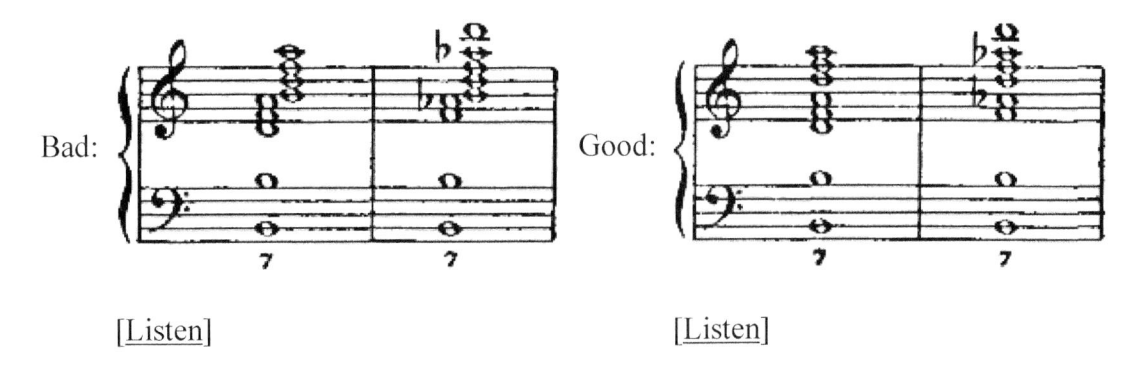

Bad: Good:

[Listen]   [Listen]

The rules of harmony concerning sustained and pedal passages apply with equal force to orchestral writing. As regards passing and auxiliary notes, *échappées*, considerable licence is permitted in rapid passages of different texture:

One texture:

A different one:

[Listen]

One texture:

A different one:

[Listen]

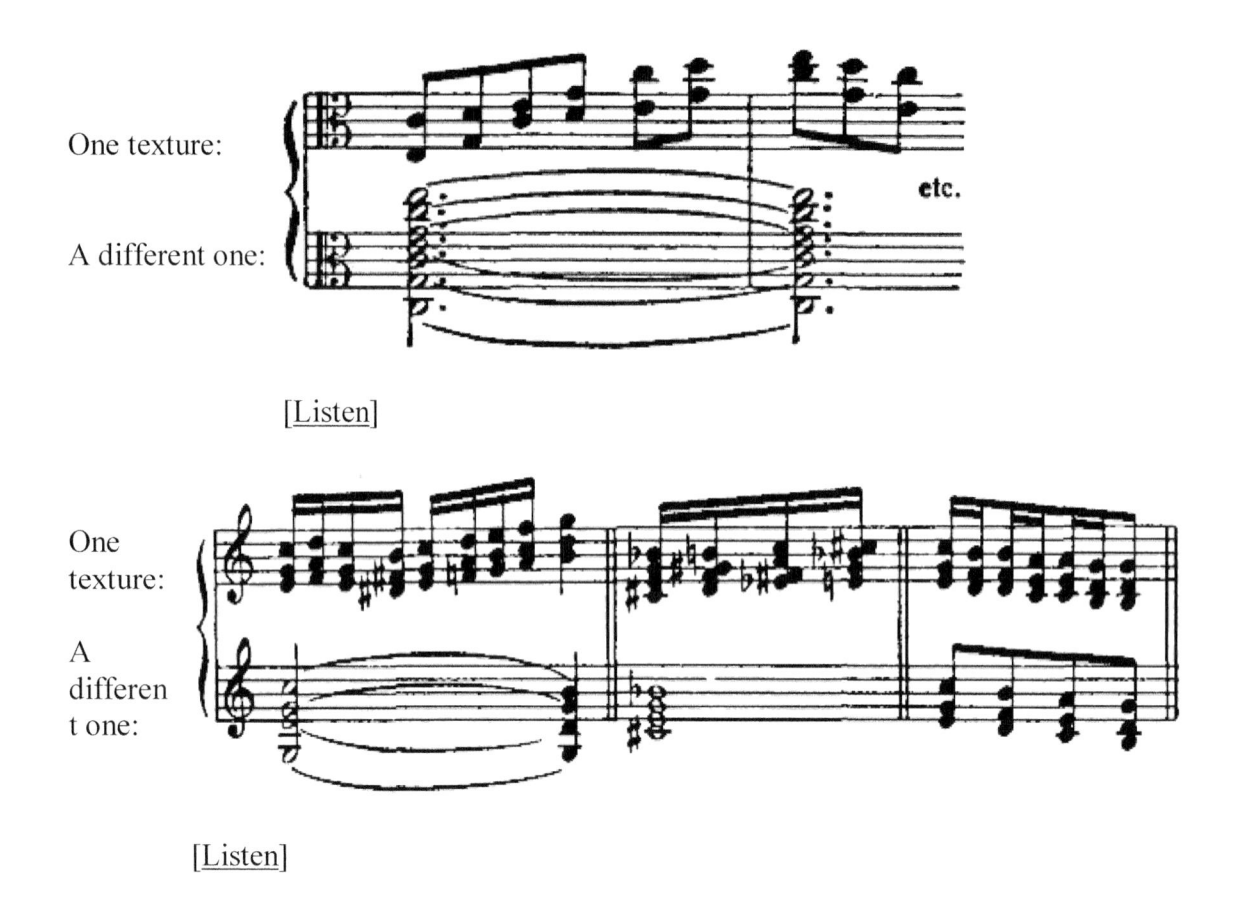

A certain figure and its essentials, in simplified form, may proceed concurrently, as in the following example:

One texture:

A different one:

A third:

[Listen]

Upper and inner pedal notes are more effective on the orchestra than in pianoforte or chamber music, owing to the greater variety of tone colour:

[Listen]

-67-

In Vol. II of the present work many examples of the above methods will be found.

Distribution of notes in chords.

The normal order of sounds or the natural harmonic scale:

[Listen]

may serve as a guide to the orchestral arrangement of chords. It will be seen that the widely-spaced intervals lie in the lower part of the scale, gradually becoming closer as the upper register is approached:

[Listen]

The bass should rarely lie at a greater distance than an octave from the part directly above it (tenor harmony). It is necessary to make sure that the harmonic notes are not lacking in the upper parts:

To be avoided:

[Listen]

The use of sixths in the upper parts, and the practice of doubling the upper note in octaves are sometimes effective methods:

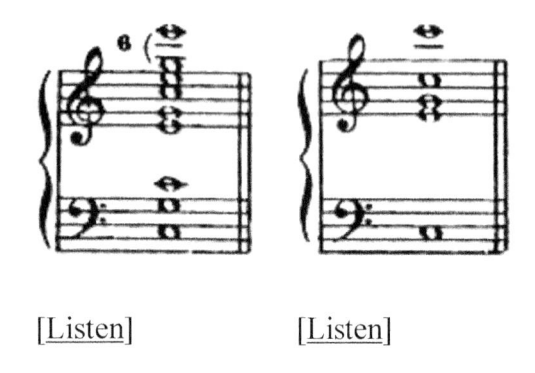

[Listen]   [Listen]

-68-

When correct progression increases the distance between the top and bottom notes of the upper parts, this does not matter:

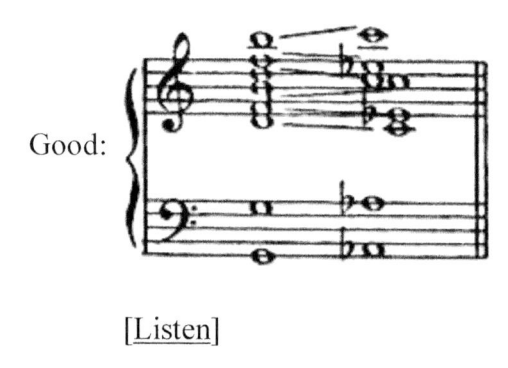

Good:

[Listen]

But it would be distinctly bad to fill in the second chord thus:

76

Not good:

[Listen]

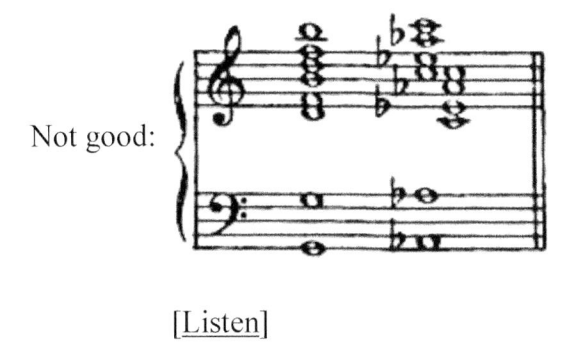

Hence it follows that the distribution of intermediate parts is a question of the greatest importance. Nothing is worse than writing chords, the upper and lower parts of which are separated by wide, empty intervals, especially in *forte* passages; in *piano* passages such distribution may be possible. Progression in contrary motion, the upper and lower parts diverging by degrees gives rise to the gradual addition of extra parts occupying the middle register:

Schematic Example:

[Listen]

When the voices converge, the middle parts are eliminated one by one:

Schematic Example:

[Listen]

-69-

String harmony.

It is an incontrovertible rule that the resonance of different harmonic parts must be equally balanced, but this balance will be less noticeable in short sharp chords than in those which are connected and sustained. Both these cases will be studied separately. In the first case, in order to increase the number of harmonic parts, each instrument in the string group may be provided with double notes or chords of three and four notes. In the second case, the resources are limited to double notes *unis*, or division of parts.

A. *Short chords.* Chords of three or four notes can only be executed rapidly on the strings.

Note. It is true that the two upper notes of a chord can be sustained and held a long time; this, however, involves complications and will be considered later.

Short chords, *arco*, only sound well when played *forte* (*sf*), and when they can be supported by wind instruments. In the execution of double notes and chords of three and four notes on the strings, balance, perfect distribution of tone, and correct progression of parts are of minor importance. What must be considered before everything is the resonance of the chords themselves, and the degree of ease with which they can be played. Those comprising notes on the gut strings are the most powerful. Chords played on several strings are usually assigned to 1st and 2nd violins and violas, the different notes being divided between them according to ease in execution and the demands of resonance. On account of its low register the 'cello is rarely called upon to play chords on three or four strings, and is usually allotted the lowest note of the chord in company with the double bass. Chords on the latter instrument are even more uncommon, but it may supply the octave on an uncovered string.

Examples:

No. 97. *Snegourotchka* 171; cf. also before 140 and before 200.

* *Spanish Capriccio*, before V (cf. Ex. 67).

Shéhérazade, 2nd movement P (cf. Ex. 19.)

* No. 98. *Tsar Saltan* 135; cf. also 141 and before 182.-70-

Isolated chords may be added to a melodic figure in the upper part, accentuating, *sforzando*, certain rhythmical moments.

Example:

No. 99. *Snegourotchka*, before 126; cf. also 326.

B. *Sustained and tremolando chords.* Chords sustained for a shorter or longer period of time, or tremolando passages, often used as a substitute, demand perfect balance of tone. Taking for granted that the different members of the string group are equal in power, the parts being written according to the usual order of register, (cf. Chap. I), it is patent that a passage in close four-part harmony, with the bass in octaves will also be uniformly resonant. When it is necessary to introduce notes to fill up the empty middle register, the upper parts being farther distant from the bass, doubled notes on the violins or violas should be used, or on both instruments together. The method of dividing strings, which is sometimes adopted, should be avoided in such cases, as certain parts of the chord will be divided and others will not; but, on the other hand, if a passage in six and seven-part harmony be written entirely for strings divided in the same manner, the balance of tone will be completely satisfactory, e.g.,

div. { Vns I / Vns I

div. { Vns II / Vns II

div. { Violas I / Violas II

If the harmony in the three upper parts, thus strengthened, is written for divided strings, the 'cellos and basses, playing *non divisi* will prove a trifle heavy; their tone must therefore be eased, either by marking the parts down or reducing the number of players.

In the case of sustained chords or *forte tremolando* on two strings, the progression of parts is not always according to rule, the intervals chosen being those which are the easiest to play.

Examples:

No. 100. *The Christmas Night* 161—Full *divisi*.

No. 101. " " " 210.—

Violas div. / 'Cellos div. } 4 part harmony.

-71-

No. 102. *Snegourotchka* 187-188—Four-part harmony, Vns I, Vns II, Violas and Violoncellos.

" 243—4 Solo 'cellos *divisi*.

Shéhérazade, 2nd movement, beginning.—4 D. bass soli div. (cf. Ex. 40).

79

The Tsar's Bride 179—Chords on all strings (cf. Ex. 243).

No. 103. *Legend of Kitesh* 8—Harmonic basis in the strings.

" " " 240—(Cf. Ex. 21).

" " " 283—Harmonic basis in the strings (cf. Ex. 2).

No. 104. *The Golden Cockerel* 4—Basis in the strings.

" " " 125—Undulating rhythm in the strings as harmonic basis (cf. Ex. 271).

In a *forte* or *sfp* chord, where one or two of the upper notes is held, either sustained or *tremolando*, the balance of tone must still be maintained, as in the following example:

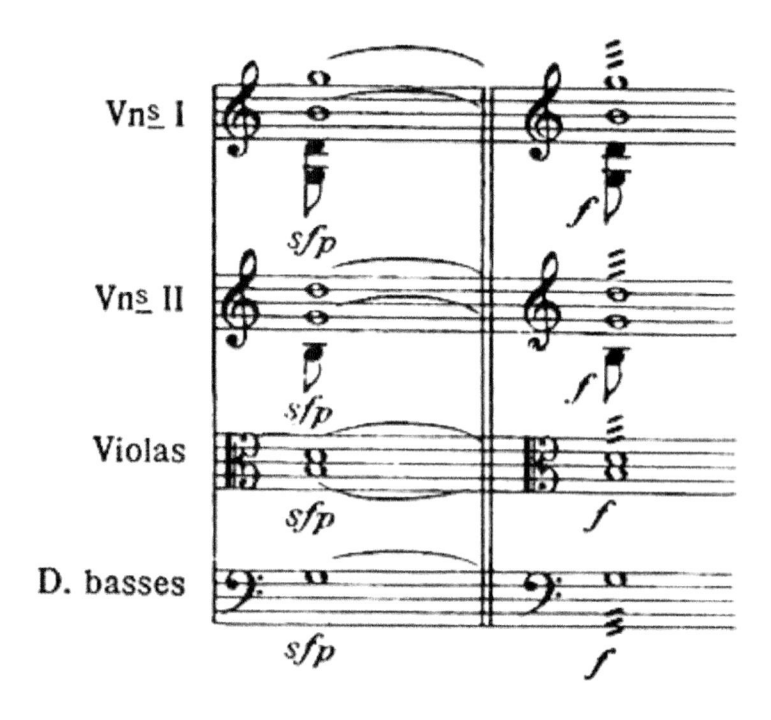

[Listen]

Wood-wind harmony.

Before entering upon this section of the work I would remind the reader of the general principles laid down in the beginning of the chapter.

Harmonic texture, composed of plain chords or ornamental designs, simple or contrapuntal in character, must possess a resonance equally distributed throughout. This may be obtained by the following means:-72-

1. Instruments forming chords must be used continuously in the same way during a given passage, that is to say they must be doubled or not throughout, except when one of the harmonic parts is to be made prominent:

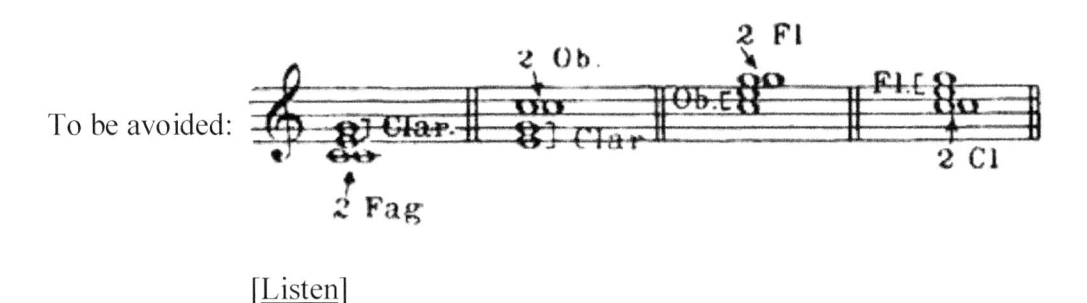

To be avoided:

[Listen]

2. The normal order of register must be followed, except in the case of crossing or enclosure of parts, which will be discussed later on:

To be avoided:

[Listen]

3. Corresponding or adjacent registers should be made to coincide except for certain colour effects:

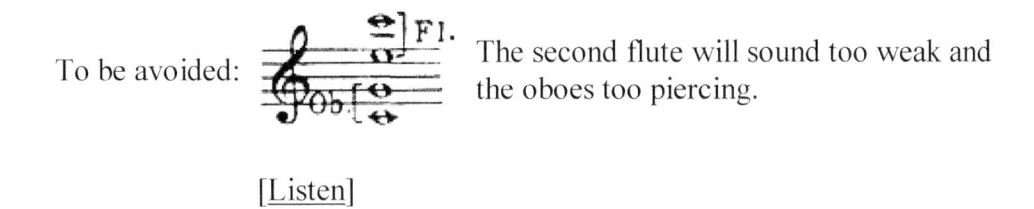

To be avoided: The second flute will sound too weak and the oboes too piercing.

[Listen]

4. Concords (octaves, thirds and sixths) and not discords (fifths, fourths, seconds and sevenths), should be given to instruments of the same kind or colour, except when discords are to be emphasised. This rule should be specially observed in writing for the oboe with its penetrating quality of tone:

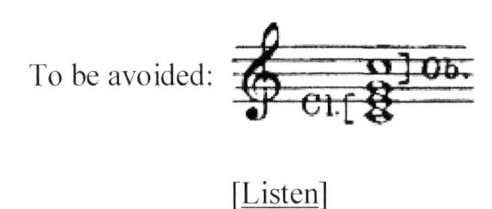

To be avoided:

[Listen]

Four-part and three-part harmony.

Harmonic writing for the wood-wind may be considered from two points of view: a) instruments in pairs, 2 Fl., 2 Ob., 2 Cl., 2 Fag.; and b) instruments in three's, 3 Fl., 2 Ob., Eng. horn, 3 Cl., 2 Fag., C-fag.

A. *In pairs.* There are three ways of distribution: 1. *Superposition* or *overlaying* (strictly following the normal order of register),-73- 2. *Crossing*, and 3. *Enclosure* of parts. The last two methods involve a certain disturbance of the natural order of register:

Overlaying. Crossing. Enclosure.

[Listen]

In choosing one of these three methods the following points must not be forgotten: a) the register of a particular isolated chord; the soft and weak register of an instrument should not be coupled with the powerful and piercing range of another:

Overlaying.   Crossing.   Enclosure.

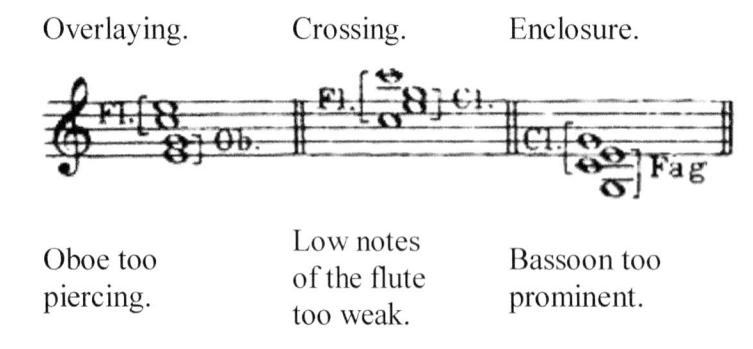

Oboe too piercing.   Low notes of the flute too weak.   Bassoon too prominent.

[Listen]

b) In a succession of chords the general progression of parts must be considered; one tone quality should be devoted to the stationary and another to the moving parts:

[Listen]

When chords are in widely-divided four-part harmony notes may be allotted in pairs to two different tone qualities, adhering to the normal order of register:

Good: [musical example] etc.

[Listen]

Any other distribution will result unquestionably in a grievous lack of relationship between registers:

To be avoided: [musical example] etc.

[Listen]

-74-

If one tone quality is to be enclosed, it must be between two different timbres:

Good: [musical example] etc.

[Listen]

It is possible to lend four distinct timbres to a chord in widely-divided four-part harmony, though such a chord will possess no uniformity in colour; but the higher the registers of the different instruments are placed, the less perceptible becomes the space which separates them:

[musical example]

Fairly good   Better   Still better

[Listen]

The use of four different timbres in close four-part harmony is to be avoided, as the respective registers will not correspond:

Bad   Better   Still slightly better

[Listen]

Note. In *Mozart and Salieri*, which is only scored for 1 Fl., 1 Ob., 1 Cl. and 1 Fag., wood-wind chords in four-part harmony are of necessity devoted to these four different timbres.

The same rules apply to writing in three-part harmony, which is the most customary form when it is a question of establishing a harmonic basis, the lowest register of which is entrusted to another group of instruments (strings *arco* or *pizz.*, for example). Chords in three-part harmony are generally given to two instruments of one timbre and a third instrument of another, but never to three different timbres. Overlaying of parts is the best course to adopt:

etc.

[Listen]

-75-

The use of crossing and enclosure of parts (which in a way amount to the same thing) must depend on the manner of their progression:

Enclosure:

[Listen]

B. *Wood-wind in three's.* Here the distribution of chords in close three-part harmony is self-evident; any grouping of three instruments of the same timbre is sure to sound well:

[Listen]

also:

[Listen]

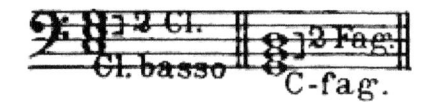

[Listen]

Overlaying of parts is the best method to follow in writing close four-part harmony; three instruments of the same timbre with a fourth instrument of another. Crossing and enclosure of parts may also be employed. Correspondence of timbres and the progression of remote parts must be kept in mind:

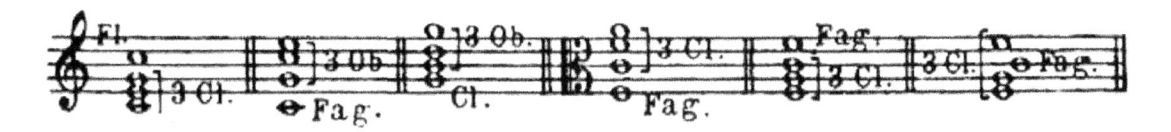

[Listen]

The method of using three instruments of the same timbre in widely-divided three-part harmony is inferior:

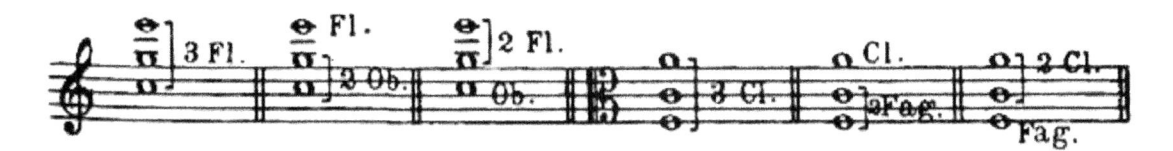

Not good Better Better Not good Better Better

85

[Listen]

-76-

But if the third instrument is of low register (Bass Fl., Eng. horn, Bass cl., or C-fag.), the resonance will be satisfactory:

[Listen]

In chords of four-part harmony, three instruments of the same timbre should be combined with a fourth instrument of another:

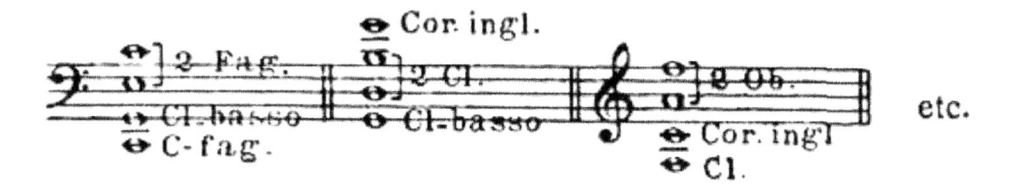

etc.

[Listen]

Harmony in several parts.

In writing chords of 5, 6, 7 and 8 part-harmony, whether they are independent, or constitute the harmonic basis, the student should follow the principles outlined in the previous chapter, dealing with the progression of wood-wind instruments in octaves. As the 5th, 6th, 7th and 8th notes are only duplications in octaves of lower notes of the real harmony (in 4 parts), instruments should be chosen which combine amongst themselves to give the best octaves. The process of crossing and enclosure of parts may also be used.

A. Wood-wind in pairs (close distribution):

[Listen]

In widely-divided harmony chords in several parts are to be avoided as they will entail both close and extended writing:

[Listen]

Note. In the majority of cases this distribution is employed when the two upper harmonic parts have a special melodic duty to perform—this question is discussed above.

-77-

B. Wood-wind in three's:

[Listen]

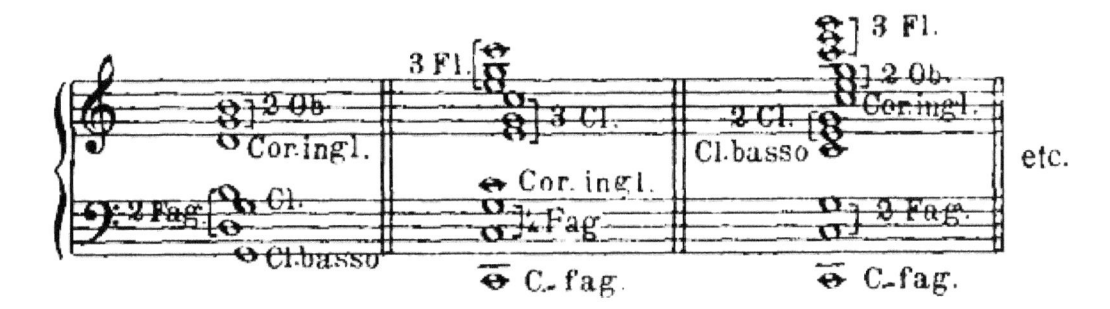

[Listen]

Overlaying of parts is the most satisfactory method in dealing with close three-part harmony. Crossing of parts is not so favourable, as octaves will be produced contrary to the natural order of register:

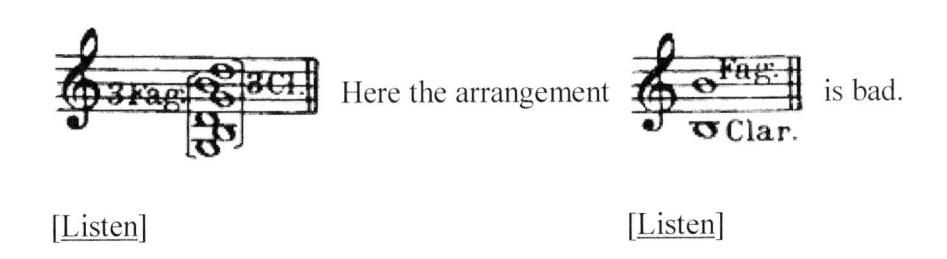

Here the arrangement is bad.

[Listen]   [Listen]

Duplication of timbres.

A. If the wood-wind is in pairs it is a good plan to mix the doubled timbres as much as possible:

Excellent

[Listen]

also:

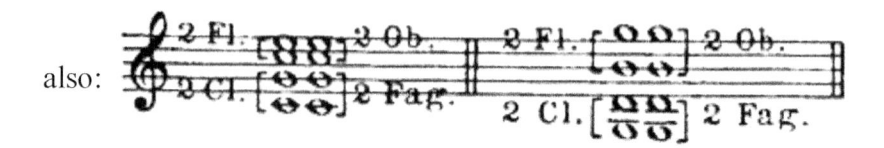

[Listen]

In chords of four-part harmony the classical method may be adopted:

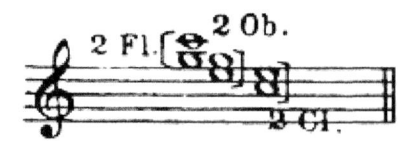

[Listen]

In this case, though the high *C* in the flute is fairly powerful, the resonance of the *G* and *E* in the oboes is softened by the duplication of the 2nd flute and 1st clarinet, while the *C* in the 2nd clarinets (not doubled) is feeble in comparison with the other notes. In any case the two extreme parts are the thinnest and weakest in tone, the intermediate parts the fullest and strongest.

B. *Wood-wind in three's* admit of perfectly balanced mixed timbres in chords of three-part harmony:

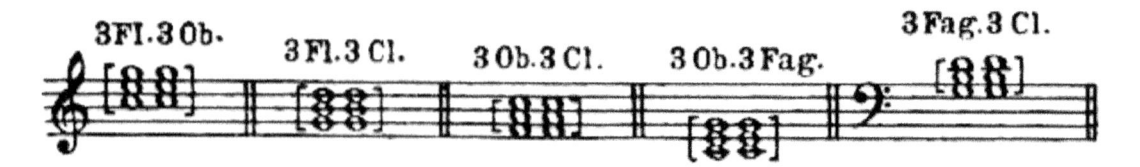

[Listen]

These timbres may even originate from three-fold duplication:

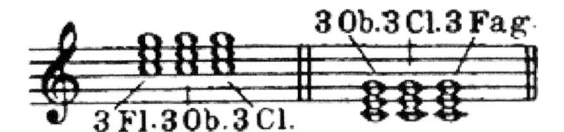

[Listen]

Remarks.

1. Modern orchestrators do not allow any void in the intermediate parts in writing close harmony; it was permitted to some extent by the classics:

[Listen]

These empty spaces create a bad effect especially in *forte* passages. For this reason widely-divided harmony, which is fundamentally based on the extension of intervals, can be used but seldom and only in *piano* passages. Close writing is the more frequent form in all harmony devoted to the wood-wind, *forte* or *piano*.

2. As a general rule a chord of greatly extended range and in several parts is distributed according to the order of the natural scale, with wide intervals (octaves and sixths), in the bass part, lesser intervals (fifths and fourths) in the middle, and close intervals (3rds or 2nds) in the upper register:-79-

[Listen]

3. In many cases correct progression of parts demands that one of them should be temporarily doubled. In such cases the ear is reconciled to the brief overthrow of balance

for the sake of a single part, and is thankful for the logical accuracy of the progression. The following example will illustrate my meaning:

[Listen]

In the second bar of this example the *D* is doubled in unison on account of the proximity of the three upper parts to their corresponding parts an octave lower. In the fourth bar the *F* is doubled in unison in both groups.

4. The formation of the harmonic basis, which is essentially in four parts, does not by any means devolve upon the wood-wind alone. One of the parts is often devoted to the strings, *arco* or *pizz*. More frequently the bass part is treated separately, the chords of greater value in the three upper parts being allotted to the wood-wind. Then, if the upper part is assigned to a group of strings, there remains nothing for the wind except the sustained harmony in the two middle parts. In the first case the three-part harmony in the wood-wind should form an independent whole, receiving no assistance from the bass; in this manner intervals of open fourths and fifths will be obviated. In the second case it is desirable to provide the intermediate parts with a moderately full tone, choosing no other intervals except seconds, sevenths, thirds or sixths.

All that has been said with regard to the use of wood-wind in the formation of harmony, and the division of simple and mixed-80- timbres applies with equal force to sustained chords, or harmonic progressions interchanging rapidly with *staccato* chords. In short chords, separated by rests of some importance, the arrangement and division of timbres is not so perceptible to the ear, and progression of parts attracts less attention. It would be useless, nay, impossible to examine the countless combinations of tone colour, all the varieties of duplication and distribution of chords. It has been my aim to denote the fundamental principles upon which to work, and to indicate the general rules to be followed. Once having mastered these, if the student devote a little time to the study of full scores, and listen to them on the orchestra, he will soon learn when certain methods should be used and when to adopt others. The pupil is advised, generally, to write for wood-wind in its normal order of distribution, to take heed that each particular chord is composed entirely either of duplicated or non-duplicated parts, (except in certain cases resulting from progression), to use the methods of crossing and enclosure of timbres with full knowledge of what he is doing, and finally to concentrate his attention on close part-writing.

Examples of wood-wind harmony:

a) Independent chords.

No. 105. *The Christmas Night* 148—Cl., 2 Fag.

No. 106. """beginning—Ob., Cl., Fag. (crossing of parts).

Snegourotchka 16—2 Cl., Fag.

"79, 5th bar.—2 Ob., 2 Fag. (cf. Ex. 136).

* No. 107. *Snegourotchka* 197—Picc., 2 Fl. (*tremolando*).

No. 108. "204—2 Fl., 2 Ob. (high register).

No. 109. *Shéhérazade*, beginning—Total wood-wind in different distribution.

* *Russian Easter Fête* A—3 Fl. *tremolando* (cf. Ex. 176).

* *Tsar Saltan* 45 Ob., 2 Fag.

No. 110. *Tsar Saltan*, before 115—mixed timbres.

No. 111. ""115, and other similar passages—very sweet effect of wood-wind in three's.

""177—2 Ob., 2 Fag.

-81-

Sadko, Symphonic Tableau 9—Ob., 2 Cl., Fag.

* *Sadko*, Opera 4—Eng. horn, 2 Cl.

""before 5—Total wood-wind.

No. 112. *Sadko* 72—Chords in three-part harmony; simple and mixed timbres.

* No. 113. *The Tsar's Bride* 126 Full wind.

* No. 114. *Legend of Kitesh*, before 90—Enclosure of parts (Ob. I in the high register).

No. 115. """before 161—Wind and brass alternately.

No. 116. """167—Full wind except oboe, with chorus.

Legend of Kitesh 269—Fl., Cl., Fag.

* *The Golden Cockerel* 125—Various wind instruments, 4 part harmony (cf. Ex. 271).

"""218—Ob., Eng. horn, Fag., C-fag.; cf. also 254.

No. 117. *The Golden Cockerel*, before 236—Mixed timbre; 2 Fag. form the bass.

b) Harmonic basis (sometimes joined by the horns).

The May Night, Act III L—2 Fag., Eng. horn (cf. Ex. 18).

Antar 68—3 Flutes.

Snegourotchka 20—2 Cl., high register.

"before 50—2 Fl., Fag.

"187—2 Ob., 2 Fag.

"274—2 Cl., low register (cf. Ex. 9).

"283—Fl., Eng. horn, Cl., Fag. (cf. Ex. 26).

No. 118. *Snegourotchka* 292—Widely-divided harmony and doubling of parts in the wind.

No. 119."318-319—2 Flutes.

Shéhérazade, 2nd movement B—2 Cl., Fag. (sustained note in the horn) (cf. Ex. 1).

The Christmas Night 1—3 Cl.

Sadko 1—Cl., Bass Cl., Fag., C-fag.

No. 120. *Sadko* 49—Ob., Cl., Horn, Fag.

"99—2 Cl. (cf. Ex. 289, 290).

-82-

No. 121. *Sadko* 144—Cl., Fag.

No. 122."195-196—2 Cl., Bass Cl.

The Tsar's Bride 80—Cl., Fag.

"""166—harmonic parts in motion, Fl. and Cl. (cf. Ex. 22).

Servilia 59—Cl. (low. register), Fag.

* No. 123. *Kashtcheï the Immortal* 80—Ob., Fag. muted.

* No. 124. *Legend of Kitesh.* 52—Fl., Fag.

"""55—Fl., Ob. (cf. Ex. 197).

"""68—Eng. horn, Fag., C-fag. (cf. Ex. 199).

No. 124."""118—mixed timbre: 2 Ob., Eng. horn and 3 Cl.

"""136—harmonic parts in motion:

"""before 185—3 Fl. (low register) and 2 Cl.

"""223—Fl., Ob., Cl. (cf. Ex. 31).

* No. 125."""247—2 Cl., Bass Cl.

"""273—Eng. horn, 2 Cl. and Bass Cl., Fag.

* No. 126."""355—Eng. horn muted, Cl., 2 Fag.

* No. 127. *The Golden Cockerel* 3—Cl., Bass Cl., Fag., C-fag.

"""40-41 Bass Cl., Fag.; Fl., Cl.; Cl., Bass Cl.

* No. 128."""156—harmonic parts in motion: Fl. and Cl.

Harmony in the brass.

Here, as in the wood-wind, part writing should be of the close order with no empty spaces in the intervals.

Four-part writing.

It is evident that the quartet of horns presents every facility for four-part harmony, perfectly balanced in tone, without doubling the bass in octaves:-83-

[Listen]

Note. In the diagrams of the present section the actual sounds of horns and trumpets are given, as in a piano score, for the sake of simplicity.

When it is found necessary to double the bass in octaves, the too resonant trombone and tuba are seldom used, the duplication being effected by the bassoon, as explained further on. The quartet of trombones and tuba is not often employed in close four-part harmony; the third trombone and the tuba usually form the bass in octaves, and the three upper parts are generally allotted to the two remaining trombones reinforced by a trumpet or two horns in unison, so as to obtain a perfect balance of tone:

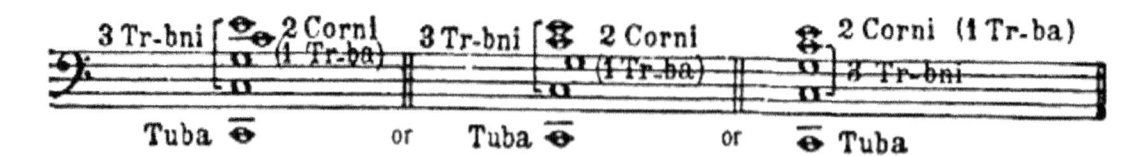

[Listen]

I have often adopted the following combination of brass instruments, and consider it eminently satisfactory: 2 horns and tuba to form the bass in octaves, the three other parts given to the trombones:

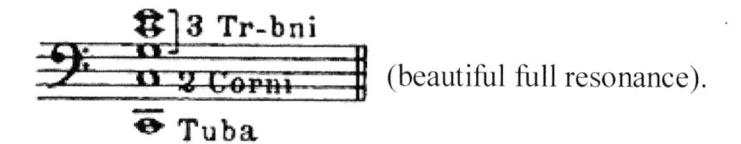

(beautiful full resonance).

[Listen]

In the higher registers, four-part harmony, of which the two upper parts are given to the trumpets, may be completed by two trombones or four horns in pairs:

[Listen]

When 3 trumpets are available the fourth part should be allotted to one trombone, or two horns in unison:

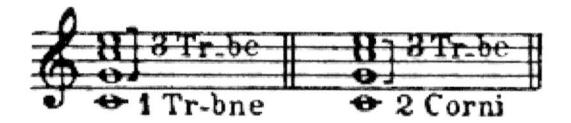

[Listen]

Enclosure of parts may be used in single chords:

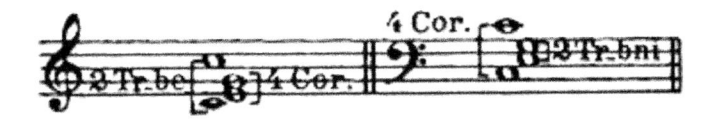

[Listen]

-84-

or in progression:

[Listen]

Three-part writing.

The best combination is trombones, horns, or trumpets in three's. If the instruments are mixed the number of horns should be doubled:

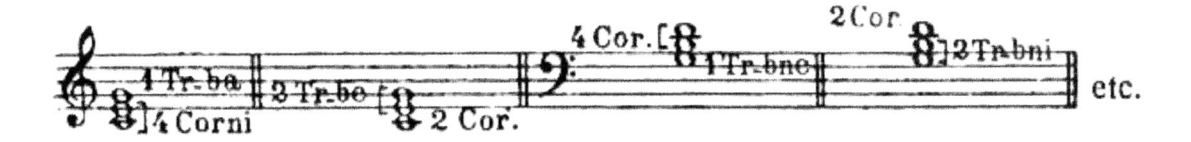

[Listen]

Writing in several parts.

When the whole group is used the number of horns should be doubled:

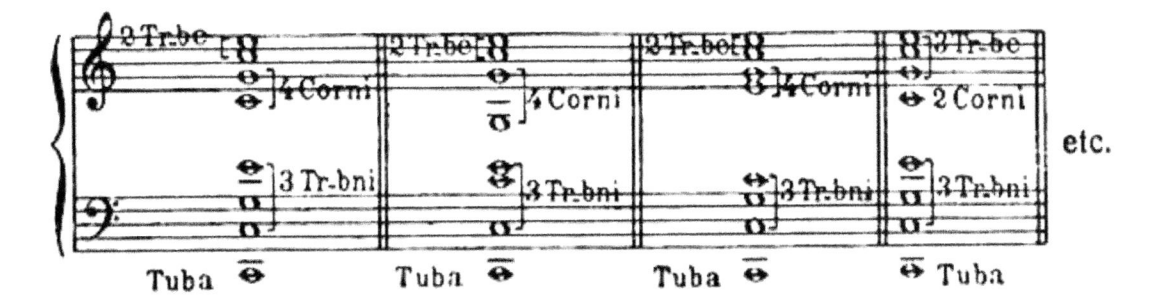

[Listen]

In seven, six, or five-part harmony certain instruments must be omitted:

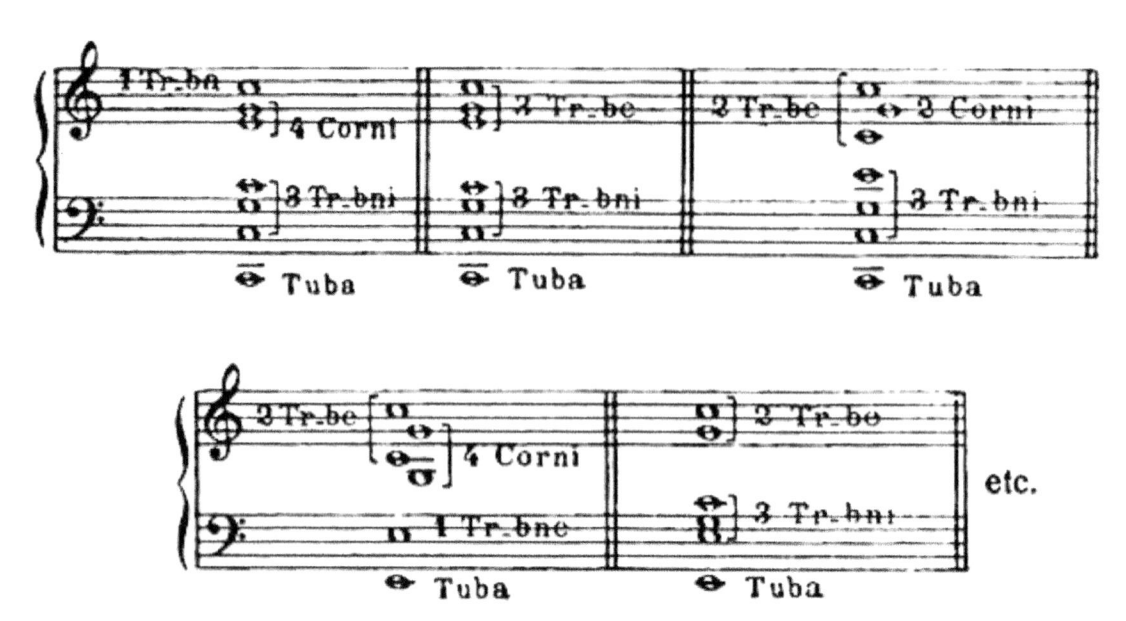

[Listen]

Discords of the seventh or second are preferably entrusted to instruments of different tone colour:-85-

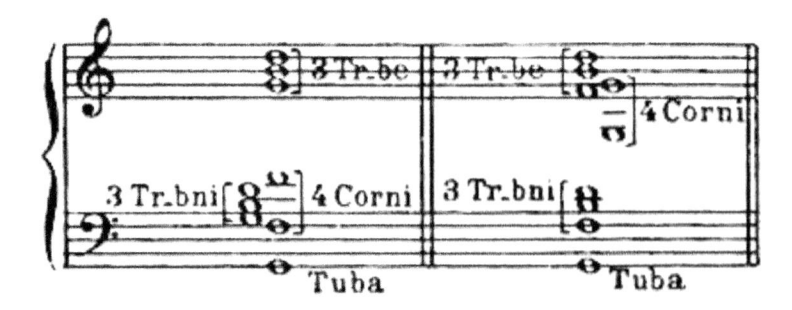

[Listen]

When such chords are written for an orchestra which only includes two trumpets, it is impossible for the horns to proceed in pairs. In such cases the following arrangement may obtain, the horns being marked one degree louder than the other instruments, to secure balance of tone:

[Listen]

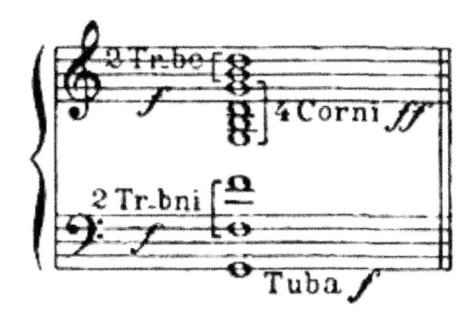

The same method should be followed whenever the use of horns in pairs fails to produce satisfactory tone.

When chords of widely-divided harmony are distributed throughout several harmonic registers, the register occupied by the horns need not be doubled; the arrangement of the chord will resemble that of a chorale written for double or triple choir. For example:

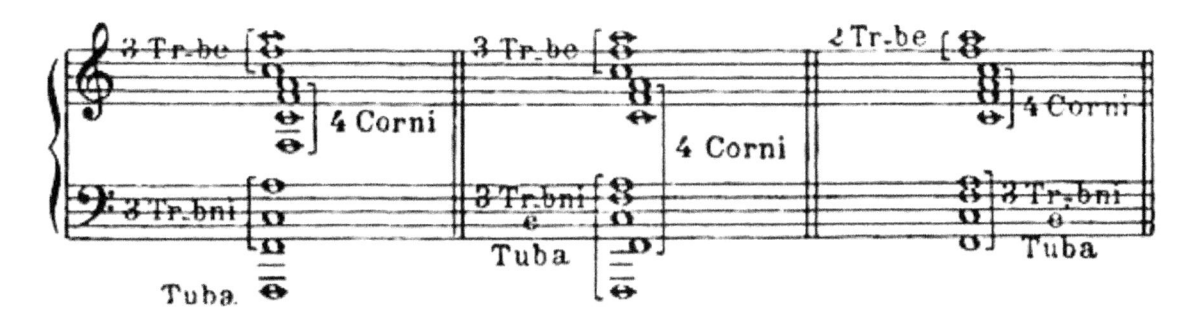

[Listen]

Duplication in the brass.

Duplication in the brass group is most frequently effected by placing a chord for horns side by side with the same chord written for trumpets or trombones. The soft round quality of the horns intensifies the tone, and moderates the penetrating timbre of the trumpets and trombones:-86-

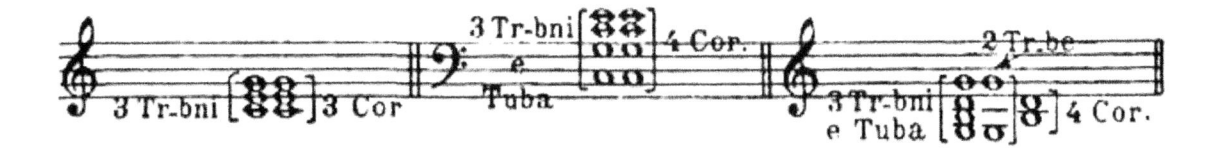

[Listen]

Similar juxtaposition of trumpets and trombones:

[Listen]

is not so common, as this unites the two most powerful agents in the group.

In handling an orchestra the brass is frequently employed to sustain notes in two or three octaves; this sphere of activity must not be ignored. The *tenuto* is generally given to two trumpets, or to two or four horns in the octave, (in double octaves). The octave is sometimes formed by trumpets and horns acting together:

[Listen]

The trombone with its ponderous tone rarely takes part in such combinations. Sustained notes in double octaves are usually apportioned thus:

[Listen]

The imperfect balance arising from the duplication of the middle note is compensated for by the mixture of timbres, which lends some unity to the chord.

Examples of harmony in the brass:

a) Independent chords:

Snegourotchka 74—3 Trombones, 2 Horns.

"140—3 Trombones, 2 Horns. Chords in different groups alternately (cf. Ex. 244).

"171—Full brass; further on 3 Trombones (cf. Ex. 97).

"255—4 Horns (stopped). -87-

No. 129. *Snegourotchka*, before 289—4 Horns.

"289—Full brass.

* *Sadko*, before 9—Full brass (enclosure of parts).

No. 130. *Sadko* 175—Mixed timbres (juxtaposition) 3 Horns + 3 Trumpets.

"before 338—Full brass except Tuba.

No. 131. "191-193 (Full brass).

No. 132. *The Christmas Night*, before 180—Full muted brass.

"""181—4 Horns + 3 Trombones + Tuba (cf. Ex. 237).

* *The Tsar's Bride* 178—Strings and brass alternately (cf. Ex. 242).

* No. 133. *Tsar Saltan* 102, 7th bar.—2 Trumpets, 2 Trombones + 4 Horns (juxtaposition).

""230—Full brass, thickly scored (cf. Table of chords No. II at the end of Vol. II, Ex. 12).

* *Servilia* 154—Various brass instruments.

* *Legend of Kitesh* 130—3 Trumpets, Trombone and Tuba.

No. 134. *Legend of Kitesh* 199—Short chords (juxtaposition).

* No. 135. *The Golden Cockerel* 115—Horns, Trombones (enclosure).

b) Harmonic basis:

No. 136. *Snegourotchka* 79, 6th bar.—4 Horns.

"231—3 Trombones, soft and sweet (cf. Ex. 8).

Antar 64-65—4 Horns; later 3 Trombones (cf. Ex. 32).

* *Shéhérazade*, 1st movement, A, E, H, K, M—Harmonic bases of different power and timbre (cf. Ex. 192-195).

No. 137. *Servilia* 93—Full brass.

* No. 138. *Tsar Saltan* 127—4 muted Horns + 3 Trombones and Tuba *con sord. pp.*

""before 147—Full brass *ff* (the 2 Oboes and Eng. horn are of no particular importance).

* *Pan Voyevoda* 136, 9th bar.—4 Horns, then Trombones, 2 Horns.

* No. 139. *Legend of Kitesh* 158—Trumpets, Trombones.

No. 140."""248—3 Trombones.

"""before 362—Full brass.

-88-

Harmony in combined groups.

A. Combination of wind and brass.

Wind and brass instruments may be combined by the method of placing a chord in one timbre side by side with the same chord in another timbre, or by any of the three methods already described: overlaying, crossing and enclosure of parts.

1. *In unison (juxtaposition or contrast of tone qualities).*

This class of combination possesses the same features as combinations in the melodic line (cf. Chap. II). Wood-wind reinforces the brass, softens it and reduces its characteristic qualities. Arrangements such as the following are possible:

2 Trumpets + 2 Fl.; 2 Trumpets + 2 Ob.; 2 Trumpets + 2 Cl.
3 Trumpets + 3 Fl.; 3 Trumpets + 3 Ob.; 3 Trumpets + 3 Cl.

Also

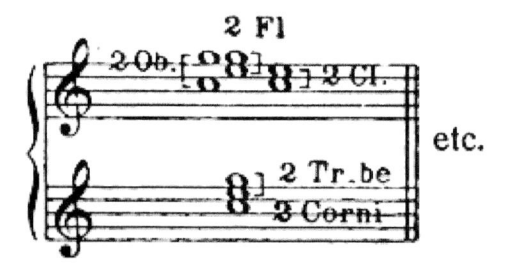

[Listen]

as well as:

2 Horns + 2 Fag.; 2 Horns + 2 Cl.;
3 Horns + 3 Fag.; 3 Horns + 3 Cl.; and:

2 Horns + 2 Fag. + 2 Cl. etc.

The combinations 3 Trombones + 3 Fag., or 3 Trombones + 3 Cl. are very rare.

A chord scored for full brass doubled by the same chords scored for full wood-wind (in pairs) produces a magnificent and uniform tone.

Examples:

Snegourotchka 315—2 Horns + 2 Cl. and 2 Horns + 2 Ob. (cf. Ex. 236).

No. 141. *The Tsar's Bride* 50—4 Horns + 2 Cl., 2 Fag.

No. 142. """142—Juxtaposition of full wind and brass.

Ivan the Terrible, Act II 30—Juxtaposition and enclosure (cf. Table of chords II, Ex. 8).

No. 143. *The Christmas Night* 165—4 Horns + Fl., Cl., Fag.-89-

* No. 144. *Sadko*, before 79—Horn, Trumpet + doubled wood-wind.[15]

No. 145."242—Full brass + Fl., Cl.

Legend of Kitesh, beginning—Horn, Trombones + Cl., Fag. (cf. also 5—Ex. 249).

* No. 146. *Legend of Kitesh* 10—Eng. horn, 2 Cl., Fag. *legato* + 4 Horns non legato.

"""324—Full brass + wind.

* No. 147. *The Golden Cockerel* 233—

Trumpets + Ob.
Horn + Cl.   ] 8.

Stopped or muted notes in trumpets and horns resemble the oboe and Eng. horn in quality; the combination of these instruments produces a magnificent tone.

Examples:

No. 148. *Russian Easter Fête*, p. 11.—Horn (+), Trumpets (low register) + Ob., Cl.

* *The Christmas Night*, before 154—Full muted brass + wind.

* No. 149. *Tsar Saltan* 129—2 Ob., Eng. horn, + 3 Trumpets muted (3 Cl. at the bottom).

* No. 150.""131 17th bar.—Same combination with added horns.

* No. 151. *Antar* 7—Ob., Eng. horn, 2 Fag. + 4 Horns (+).

A beautiful dark tone is derived from the combination of middle notes in stopped horns and deep notes in the clarinet:

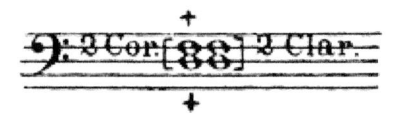

[Listen]

If bassoons are substituted for clarinets the effect loses part of its character.

Examples:

* *Kashtcheï the Immortal* 29, 11th bar,—2 Ob., 2 Cl. + 4 Horns (+).

""" 107, 6th bar.—2 Cl., Fag. + 3 Horns (+).

* *The Christmas Night*, p. 249—Cl., Fag. + 3 Horns (+).

* *Mlada*, Act III 19—3 Horns (+) + 3 Fag. and 3 Horns (+) + 3 Ob. (cf. Ex. 259).

-90-

2. *Overlaying (superposition), crossing, enclosure of parts.*

It has already been stated that the bassoon and horn are the two instruments best capable of reconciling the groups of wood-wind and brass. Four-part harmony given to two bassoons and two horns, especially in soft passages, yields a finely-balanced tone recalling the effect of a quartet of horns, but possessing slightly greater transparence. In *forte* passages the horns overwhelm the bassoons, and it is wiser to employ four horns alone. In the former case crossing of parts is to be recommended for the purposes of blend, the concords being given to the horns, the discords to the bassoons:

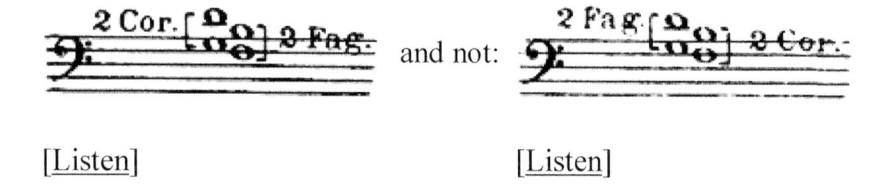

and not:

[Listen]   [Listen]

Bassoons may also be written inside the horns, but the inverse process is not to be recommended:

[Listen]

The same insetting of parts may be used for sustained trumpet notes in octaves. In soft passages, thirds played in the low register of the flutes, sometimes combined with clarinets, produce a beautiful mysterious effect between trumpets in octaves. In a chain of consecutive chords it is advisable to entrust the stationary parts to the brass, the moving parts to the wood-wind.

Clarinets, on account of their tone quality should rarely be set inside the horns, but, in the upper register, and in the higher harmonic parts, a chord of four horns, (*piano*), may be completed by clarinets as effectively as by oboes or flutes; the bassoon may then double the base an octave below:

[Listen]

Played *forte*, the horns are more powerful than the wood-wind; balance may be established by doubling the upper harmonic parts:-91-

[Listen]

Examples:

a) Superposition.

* *Sadko*, Symphonic Tableau 1, 9—Fl., Ob., Cl., Horn (basis).

"before 14—2 Fl., Cl., Horns.

"final chord—Fl., Cl., Horn.

* *Antar* 22—Fl., Cl., Horns (basis).

No. 152. *Antar* 56—3 Fl., 4 Horns (basis).

* *Snegourotchka* 300—Full wind and horns.

* *Shéhérazade*—Final chords of 1st and 4th movements.

* *Russian Easter Fête* D—Fl., Cl., Horn; later trumpets and trombones in juxtaposition (cf. Ex. 248).

* No. 153. *The Christmas Night* 212, 10th bar.—Wind and Horns; trumpets and trombones added later.

"""215

$\left.\begin{array}{l}\text{3 Fl. + 3 Cl.}\\\text{3 Horns}\end{array}\right]$ 8.

* *Sadko*, Opera 165—Juxtaposition and Superposition.

No. 154. *Sadko* 338—Same distribution.

No. 155. *Servilia* 73

3 Fl + 2 Ob., Cl.
4 Horns.

* No. 156. *Legend of Kitesh*, before 157—3 Flutes, 3 Trombones.

"""final chord (cf. Table III of chords, Ex. 15).

* *The Golden Cockerel*, before 219—Mixed timbre of wood-wind, 4 Horns.

b) Crossing.

* *The Christmas Night*, before 53—Horn, Fag.

"""107—Clar., Horn, Fag.

* *Legend of Tsar Saltan*, before 62—Horn, Fag.

* *The Golden Cockerel* 220—3 Trombones, 2 Fag., C-fag. (cf. Ex. 232).

* No. 157. *Antar*, before 30—Wood-wind, Horns, then Trumpets.-92-

c) Enclosure:

No. 158. *Ivan the Terrible*, Act I 33—Flutes within horns; later horns within bassoons.

No. 159. *Snegourotchka* 183—

Trumpet
Fl., 2 Cl.
Trumpet

* *Sadko*, symphonic tableau 3—

Cl. + Fag.
4 Horns
Cl. + Fag.

* *Antar* before 37—

Fag.
2 Horns (+)
Cl.

* *Sadko*, Opera 105—Harmonic basis; oboes within trumpets (cf. Ex. 260).

* No. 160. *Sadko*, Opera, before 155—Flutes within trumpets.

* *The Tsar's Bride*, end of Overture—Bassoons within horns (cf. Table III of chords, Ex. 14).

* No. 161. *Tsar Saltan* 50—Trumpets within wood-wind doubled.

No. 162.""59—Flutes within trumpets; clarinets within horns.

* No. 163. *Legend of Kitesh* 82—Oboes and clarinets within trumpets.

The relationship which has been shown to exist between stopped horns and oboe or Eng. horn authorizes the simultaneous use of these instruments in one and the same chord, played *p* or *sfp*:

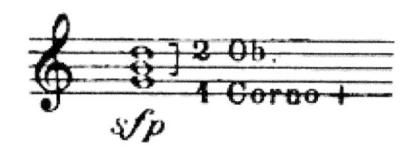

[Listen]

Examples:

* *The Christmas Night* 75—3 Horns (+) + Oboe.

The Tsar's Bride 123—Ob., Eng. horn, Horn (+) (cf. Ex. 240).

* *Legend of Kitesh* 244—Cl., 2 Fl., + 2 Ob., Eng. horn, 3 Horn (+).

* No. 164. *Legend of Kitesh*, before 256—

2 Ob., Eng. horn
3 Horns (+)] 8.

* Cf. also *Tsar Saltan*, before 115—

Horn (+)
2 Fl. + 2 Fag.   (Ex. 110).

If trumpets and trombones take part in a chord, flutes, oboes and clarinets are better used to form the harmonic part above the trumpets. The following should be the arrangement:-
93-

[Listen]

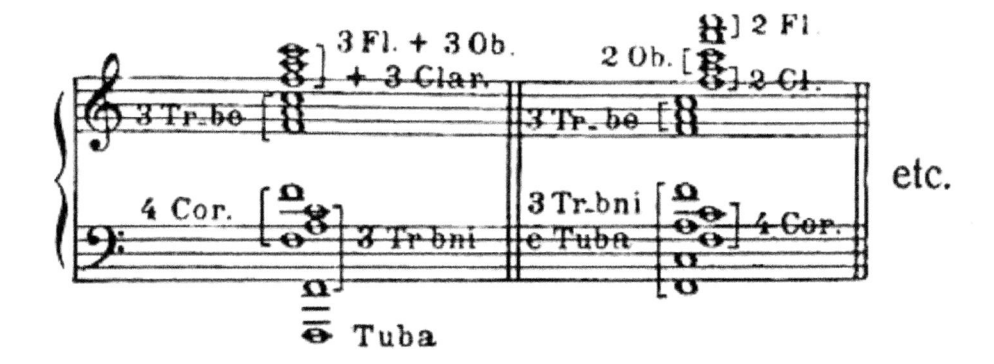

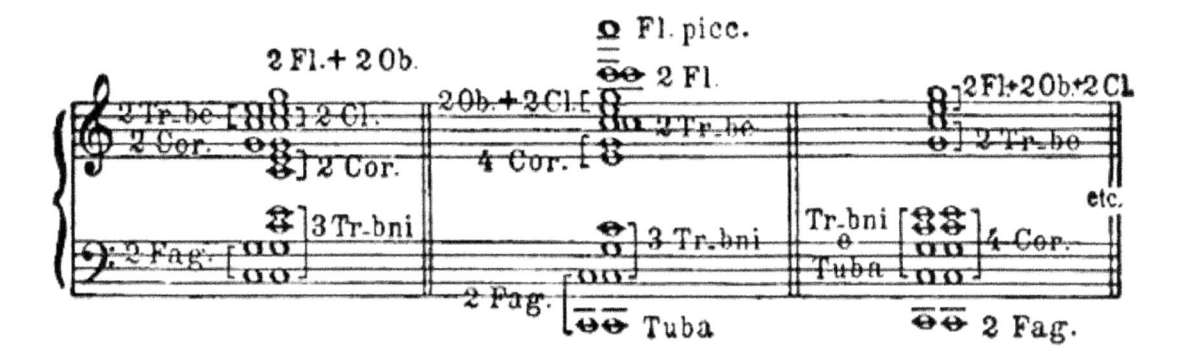

[Listen]

Examples:

* *Sadko*, symphonic tableau 20.

* No. 165. *The May Night*, Act I Ee—3 Trombones, 2 Ob. + 2 Cl. + 2 Fag.

"""p. 325.—Final chord, *C* maj. (cf. Table I of chords, Ex. 1).

* No. 166. *Snegourotchka* 198; cf. also 200 and before 210.

* *Shéhérazade*, 1st movement E, 2nd movement P, 3rd movement M, 4th movement p. 203 (cf. Ex. 195, 19, 210, 77).

No. 167. *The Christmas Night* 205; cf. also 161, 212, 14th bar. (Ex. 100, 153).

* *Mlada*, end of Act I (cf. Chord Table II, Ex. 13). Act II 20.

No. 168-169. *Sadko*, Opera, before 249, 302; cf. also Ex. 120. -94-

No. 170. *Sadko*, Opera 244—Chord of widely extended range; bassoons at the limit of low compass.

""142, 239; cf. also 3 (Ex. 86).

* *The Tsar's Bride* 179 (cf. Ex. 243).

Antar 65—Alternation of notes in horns and wood-wind on trombone chords (cf. Ex. 32).

General observations. It is not always possible to secure proper balance in scoring for full wood-wind. For instance, in a succession of chords where the melodic position is constantly changing, distribution is subordinate to correct progression of parts. In practice, however, any inequality of tone may be counterbalanced by the following acoustic phenomenon: in every chord the parts in octaves strengthen one another, the harmonic sounds in the lowest register coinciding with and supporting those in the highest. In spite of this fact it rests entirely with the orchestrator to obtain the best possible balance of tone; in difficult cases this may be secured by judicious dynamic grading, marking the wood-wind one degree louder than the brass.

B. Combination of strings and wind.

1. We frequently meet with the combination of strings and wood-wind in the light of comparison of one timbre with another, either in long sustained notes, or *tremolando* in the strings. Apart from the complete or partial doubling of the string quartet (two methods frequently used), the general and most natural arrangement is:

$$\frac{\text{Fl.}}{\text{Ob. (Cl.)}} + \text{Vns div.}; \frac{\text{Clar.}}{\text{Fag.}} + \text{'Cellos} + \text{Violas div., etc.}$$

Examples:

* *Sadko*, Symphonic Tableau before 4, and 4, 9th bar.

* *Shéhérazade*, 1st movement M 6 Vns soli + 2 Ob. (2 Fl.), Cl.

* *Antar* 7—String quartet *divisi* + wood-wind (cf. Ex. 151).

* No. 171. *Antar* 57—Vns II, Violas div. + Fl., Horn (florid accompaniment in the Clar.).

* *Legend of Kitesh* 295—the same; rhythmic motion in the wind, sustained harmony in the strings (cf. Ex. 213).-95-

2. Owing to the complete absence of any affinity in tone quality, the combination of strings with brass is seldom employed in juxtaposition, crossing, or enclosure of parts.

The first method may be used however when the harmony is formed by the strings *tremolando*, and the brass is employed in sustaining chords, also when the strings play short disconnected chords, *sforzando*. Another possible exception may be mentioned; the splendid effect of horns doubled by divided violas or 'cellos.

Examples:

Snegourotchka 242—Full brass + strings *tremolando* (cf. 1st Table of chords, Ex. 6).

* *Legend of Kitesh*, before 240—the same (Horn, Trumpet +).

* *Sadko*, Opera, before 34—Horn + Violas *div.*, Trombones + 'Cellos *div.* [16]

C. Combination of the three groups.

The combination of strings, wood-wind and brass instruments, set side by side, produces a full, round and firm tone.

Examples:

No. 172. *The Tsar's Bride*, before 145—Ob., Fag. + Horns + Strings.

"""final chord (cf. Table I of chords, Ex. 5).

* No. 173. *Sadko*, end of 1st tableau—short chords. Last chords of the 1st, 3rd and 7th tableaux (cf. Table I and III, Vol. II, Ex. 9, 10, 18).

* No. 174. *The Christmas Night* 22—Wind + Brass *c. sord.* + *tremolo* strings.

Legend of Kitesh 162 (cf. Ex. 250).

Snegourotchka—end of opera, (cf. Table III in Vol. II, Ex. 17) and a host of other examples.-96-

General Observations. Balance and correct distribution of tone is much more important in dealing with long sustained chords or those of rhythmic design; in the case of short, disconnected chords resonance is a minor consideration, but one which should not be entirely neglected.

I have endeavoured to outline the general principles to be followed, but I do not profess to deal with all the countless cases which may arise in the course of orchestration. I have given a few examples of well-sounding chords; for further information I advise the reader to study full scores with care, as this is the only method to acquire perfect knowledge of the distribution and doubling of various instruments.

Chapter IV.

COMPOSITION OF THE ORCHESTRA.

Different ways of orchestrating the same music.

There are times when the general tone, character and atmosphere of a passage, or a given moment in an orchestral work point to one, and only one particular manner of scoring. The following simple example will serve for explanation. Take a short phrase where a flourish or fanfare call is given out above a *tremolando* accompaniment, with or without change in harmony. There is no doubt that any orchestrator would assign the *tremolo* to the strings and the fanfare to a trumpet, never *vice versa*. But taking this for granted, the composer or orchestrator may still be left in doubt. Is the fanfare flourish suitable to the range of a trumpet? Should it be written for two or three trumpets in unison, or doubled by other instruments? Can any of these methods be employed without damaging the musical meaning? These are questions which I shall endeavour to answer.

If the phrase is too low in register for the trumpets it should be given to the horns (instruments allied to the trumpet); if the phrase is too high it may be entrusted to the oboes and clarinets in unison, this combination possessing the closest resemblance to the trumpet tone both in character and power. The question whether one trumpet or two should be employed must be decided by the degree of power to be vested in the given passage. If a big sonorous effect is required the instruments may be doubled, tripled, or even multiplied by four; in the opposite case one solo brass instrument, or two of the wood-wind will suffice (1 Ob. + 1 Cl.). The question whether the *tremolo* in the strings should be supported-98- by sustained harmony in the wood-wind depends upon the purpose in view. A composer realises his intentions beforehand, others who orchestrate his music can only proceed by conjecture. Should the composer desire to establish a strongly-marked difference between the harmonic basis and the melodic outline it is better not to employ wood-wind harmony, but to obtain proper balance of tone by carefully distributing his dynamic marks of expression, *pp, p, f* and *ff*. If, on the contrary, the composer desires a full round tone as harmonic basis and less show of brilliance in the harmonic parts, the use of harmony in the wood-wind is to be recommended. The following may serve as a guide to the scoring of wood-wind chords: the harmonic basis should differ from the melody not only in fullness and intensity of tone, but also in colour. If the fanfare figure is allotted to the brass (trumpets or horns) the harmony should be given to the wood-wind; if the phrase is given to the wood-wind (oboes and clarinets) the harmony should be entrusted to the horns. To solve all these questions successfully a composer must have full knowledge of the purpose he has in view, and those who orchestrate his work should be permeated with his intentions. Here the question arises, what should those intentions be? This is a more difficult subject.

The aim of a composer is closely allied to the form of his work, to the aesthetic meaning of its every moment and phrase considered apart, and in relation to the composition as a whole. The choice of an orchestral scheme depends on the musical matter, the colouring of preceding and subsequent passages. It is important to determine whether a given passage is a complement to or a contrast with what goes before and comes after, whether it forms a climax or merely a step in the general march of musical thought. It would be impossible to examine all such possible types of relationship, or to consider the *rôle* played by each passage quoted in the present work. The reader is therefore advised not to pay too much attention to the examples given, but to study them and their bearing on the context in their proper place in the full scores. Nevertheless I shall touch upon a few of these points in the course of the following outline. To begin with, young and inexperienced composers do not always possess a clear idea of what they wish to do. They can improve in this direction by reading-99- good scores and by repeatedly listening to an orchestra, provided they concentrate the mind to the fullest possible extent. The search after extravagant and daring effects in orchestration is quite a different thing from mere caprice; *the will to achieve is not sufficient; there are certain things which should not be achieved.*

The simplest musical ideas, melodic phrases in unison and octaves, or repeated throughout several octaves, chords, of which no single part has any melodic meaning are scored in various ways according to register, dynamic effect and the quality of expression or tone colour that may be desired. In many cases, one idea will be orchestrated in a different way every time it recurs. Later on I shall frequently touch upon this more complicated question.

Examples:

* *Snegourotchka* 58; 65 and before 68—sustained note in unison.

There are fewer possible ways of scoring more complex musical ideas, harmonico-melodic phrases, polyphonic designs etc.; sometimes there are but two methods to be followed, for each of the primary elements in music, melody, harmony, and counterpoint possesses its own special requirements, regulating the choice of instruments and tone colour. The most complicated musical ideas sometimes admit of only one manner of scoring, with a few hardly noticeable variations in detail. To the following example, very simple in structure I add an alternative method of scoring:

Example:

No. 175. *Vera Scheloga*, before 35—a) actual orchestration, *b)—another method.

It is obvious that the method b) will produce satisfactory tone. But a 3rd and 4th way of scoring would be less successful, and a continuation of this process would soon lead to the ridiculous. For instance if the chords were given to the brass the whole passage would sound heavy, and the soprano recitative in the low and middle register would be overpowered. If the *F* sharp in the-100- double basses were played *arco* by 'cellos and basses together it would sound clumsy, if it were given to the bassoons a comic effect would be produced, and if played by the brass it would sound rough and coarse, etc.

The object of scoring the same musical phrase in different ways is to obtain variety either in tone colour or resonance. In each case the composer may resort to the inversion of the normal order of instruments, duplication of parts, or the two processes in combination. The first of these is not always feasible. In the preceding sections of the book I have tried to explain the characteristics of each instrument and the part which each group of instruments plays in the orchestra. Moreover many methods of doubling are to be avoided; these I have mentioned, while there are also some instruments which cannot be combined owing to the great difference in their peculiarities. Therefore, as regards the general composition of the orchestra, the student should be guided by the general principles laid down in the earlier stages of the present work.

The best means of orchestrating the same musical idea in various ways is by the adaptation of the musical matter. This can be done by the following operations: a) complete or partial transference into other octaves; b) repetition in a different key; c) extension of the whole range by the addition of octaves to the upper and lower parts; d) alteration of details (the most frequent method); e) variation of the general dynamic scheme, e.g. repeating a phrase *piano*, which has already been played *forte*.

These operations are always successful in producing variety of orchestral colour.

Examples:

No. 176, 177. *Russian Easter Fête* A and C.

The Christmas Night 158 and 179.

No. 178-181. *The Tsar's Bride*, Overture: beginning, 1, 2, 7.

Sadko 99-101 and 305-307 (cf. Ex. 289, 290, and 75).

No. 182-186. *Tsar Saltan* 14, 17, 26, 28, 34.

No. 187-189.""181, 246, 220.

* No. 190-191. *Ivan the Terrible*, Overture 5 and 12.

-101-

Spanish Capriccio—compare 1st and 3rd movement.

* No. 192-195. *Shéhérazade*, 1st movement—beginning of the *allegro* A, E, M.

" 3rd movement—beginning A, I.

" 3rd" E, G, O.

* No. 196-198. *Legend of Kitesh* 55, 56, 62.

* No. 199-201.""" 68, 70, 84.

(Cf. also Ex. 213, 214. *Legend of Kitesh* 294 and 312.)

* No. 202-203. *The Golden Cockerel* 229, 233.

The process of scoring the same or similar ideas in different ways is the source of numerous musical operations, *crescendo*, *diminuendo*, interchange of tone qualities, variation of tone colour etc., and incidentally throws new light upon the fundamental composition of the orchestra.

Full *Tutti*.

The word *tutti* generally means the simultaneous use of all instruments, but the word "all" is used relatively, and it must not be inferred that every single instrument must necessarily be employed to form a *tutti*. In order to simplify the following illustrations I will divide the word into two classes, *full tutti* and *partial tutti*,—independently of whether the orchestra is constructed in pairs, in three's, or a larger number of instruments. I call *full tutti* the combination of all melodic groups, strings, wind, and brass. By *partial tutti* I mean passages in which the brass group only takes part, whether two horns or two trumpets participate alone, or whether two horns are combined with one or three trombones, without tuba, trumpets, or the two remaining horns, etc.:

4 Horns,	2 Horns or 2 Trumpets, or	2 Horns	].
[. . . .		. . . . .	etc.
. . . .	. . . . . .	3 Trombones	

In both species of *tutti* full wood-wind may be employed or not, according to the register and musical context of the passage. For instance, in the extreme high register it may be essential to include the piccolo; in the low register flutes will be unnecessary, and yet the passage can still be called *tutti*. The inclusion of kettle-drums, harp, and other instruments of little sustaining power, as of the percussion in general, does not come under discussion.-102-

The variety of orchestral operations increases with the number of instruments forming a *tutti*, in fact, so great does it become that it is impossible to consider all combinations. I can only give a few examples of full and partial *tutti*, and leave the reader to draw his own conclusions. Some of these examples fall under the double heading of full and partial *tutti*, and the student is reminded that the *tutti* is used essentially in *forte* and *fortissimo*, rarely in *pianissimo* and *piano* passages.

Examples:

Snegourotchka 61 and 62—Partial and full *Tutti*.

" 231 Partial *Tutti*, without the trumpets (cf. Ex. 8).

No. 204. *Snegourotchka* 216—Full *Tutti*.

" 325-326—Full *Tutti* and chorus (cf. Ex. 8).

Sadko 3, 223, 239—Full *Tutti* (cf. Ex. 86).

No. 205-206. *Sadko* 173, 177—Full *Tutti* with chorus, differently scored.

No. 207-208. *The Christmas Night* 184 and 186—Full *Tutti*, orchestrated in different ways, with and without chorus.

* *The Tsar's Bride*, Overture 1, 2, 7—Full and partial *Tutti* (cf. Ex. 179-181).

* """ 141—Full *Tutti*.

* """ 177— ""

Pan Voyevoda 186 and 188 Full *Tutti*.

* *Antar* 65—(cf. Ex. 32).

* No. 209. *Shéhérazade*, 3rd movement M; cf. also 1st movement A, E, H; 2nd movement K, P, R; 3rd movement G, O; 4th movement G, P, W and further on to Y (No. 193, 194, 19, 66, 77).

* *Spanish Capriccio* B, F, J, P, V, X-Z (cf. Ex. 3).

* *Russian Easter Fête* F, J, before L, Y, up to the end.

* *3rd Symphony*, 1st movement D, R-T, X; 2nd movement A, E; 4th movement A, H, S.

* *Sadko*, Symphonic tableau 20-24.

* *Mlada*, Act III 12 (cf. Ex. 258).

* For examples of *Tutti* chords, see special Tables at the end of Vol. II.-103-

Tutti in the wind.

In many cases the wood-wind and brass groups can form a *tutti* by themselves for periods of varying length. Sometimes this is effected by the wood-wind alone, but more frequently with the support of horns. At other times the horns are found alone without the wood-wind, and, lastly, a *tutti* may be comprised of instruments of each group in varying numbers. The addition of kettle-drums and the rest of the percussion is quite common and constitutes what the Germans call "Janitscharenmusik", or Turkish infantry music. Violoncellos and double basses playing more or less important *pizz.* notes are often added to wood-wind instruments (*tutti*), likewise the remainder of the strings and the harps; this process renders the sustained notes in the wood-wind more distinct. *Tutti* passages in wood-wind and horns do not produce any great amount of power in *forte* passages, but, on the other hand *tutti* in the brass groups alone may attain an extraordinary volume of tone. In the following examples the formation of pedal notes by strings or wood-wind in no way alters the general character of the *Tutti*:

Examples:

No. 210-211. *Snegourotchka* 149, 151 (compare).

Tsar Saltan 14, 17, 26 (cf. Ex. 182-184).

Pan Voyevoda 57, 186, 262.

No. 212. *Ivan the Terrible*, Act II 19; cf. also Act. III 5.

* No. 213-214. *Legend of Kitesh* 294, 312 (compare).

* No. 215. *The Golden Cockerel* 116; cf. also 82 and 84.

* *Antar* 37 (cf. Ex. 65).

Tutti pizzicato.

The quartet of strings (*pizzicato*), reinforced occasionally by the harp and piano, may, in certain cases constitute a particular kind of *tutti*, which can only attain any great degree of strength by support from the wood-wind. Without this support it is of medium power, though still fairly brilliant in quality.-104-

Examples:

No. 216. *Snegourotchka*, before 128; cf. also 153 and before 305.

* No. 217. *Russian Easter Fête* K; cf. also U and V.

* *Spanish Capriccio* A, C, before S, before P; cf. also O (Ex. 56).

Mlada, Act II 15.

* *Sadko*: 220 (cf. Ex. 295).

* *Legend of Kitesh* 101.

* No. 218. *The May Night*, Act I, The Mayor's Song—combination of strings, *arco* and *pizz*.

Tutti in one, two and three parts.

It often happens that a moderately full orchestral *ensemble* executes a passage composed of one or two harmonic parts, in unison or in octaves. Such melodic phrases call for more or less simple orchestration with the usual doubling of parts, or, in ornamental writing, admit of contrast in tone colouring, occasionally with the addition of sustained notes.

Examples:

Snegourotchka, before 152, 174, 176.

The Tsar's Bride 120-121 (cf. Ex. 63).

The Golden Cockerel 215.

* No. 219-221. *Legend of Kitesh* 142, 144, 147—3 part *Tutti*, with different scoring.

* *Legend of Kitesh* 138, 139—*Tutti* in one part.

Soli in the strings.

Although, in any orchestral piece, numerous instances are to be found of melodies and phrases entrusted to a solo wind instrument (generally the first of each group, wood-wind or brass), solos for stringed instruments, on the other hand, are extremely rare. Whilst the 1st violin and 1st 'cello are fairly frequently used in this manner, the solo viola is seldom found, and a solo on the double bass is practically unknown. Phrases demanding particular individuality-105- of expression are entrusted to solo instruments; likewise passages that require extraordinary technique, beyond the scope of the orchestral rank and file. The comparatively weak tone of the solo instrument necessitates light, transparent accompaniment. Difficult virtuoso solos should not be written, as they attract too much attention to a particular instrument. Solo stringed instruments are also used when vigourous expression and technical facility are not required, but simply in order to obtain that singular difference in colour which exists between a solo stringed instrument and strings in unison. Two solo instruments can be coupled together, e.g. 2 *Violins soli*, etc. and in very rare cases a quartet of solo strings may be employed.

Examples:

Violin solo:

No. 222-223. *Snegourotchka* 54, 275.

The May Night, pp. 64-78.

Mlada, Act I 52; Act III, before 19.

* *A Fairy Tale* W.

* *Shéhérazade*, 1st movement C, G; also the passages at the start of each movement.

* *Spanish Capriccio* H, K, R, and the cadence on p. 38.

* No. 224. *Legend of Kitesh* 310—Vn. solo, on harmonic basis of strings *sul ponticello* and wood-wind.

Snegourotchka 274, 279—2 Vns soli (cf. Ex. 9).

Viola solo:

No. 225. *Snegourotchka* 212.

Sadko 137.

* No. 226. *The Golden Cockerel* 163; cf. also 174, 177.

Violoncello solo:

Snegourotchka 187 (cf. Ex. 102).

The Christmas Night, before 29, 130.

Mlada, Act III 36.

* *The Golden Cockerel* 177, 180 (cf. Ex. 229).-106-

Double bass solo:

* No. 227. *Mlada*, Act II 10-12—a special instance where the first string is tuned down.

Solo quartet:

The Christmas Night 222—Vn., Viola, 'Cello, D. bass.

* No. 228. *Tsar Saltan* 248—Vn. I, Vn. II, Viola, 'Cello.

* The case of a solo stringed instrument doubled by the wood-wind in unison must not be forgotten. The object is to attain great purity and abundance of tone, without impairing the timbre of the solo instrument (especially in the high and low registers), or to produce a certain highly-coloured effect.

Examples:

* *Mlada*, Act II 52—Vn. + Fl.; Act IV 31—Viol. + Fl. + Harp.

* *The Christmas Night* 212—2 Vns + Fl. + Small Cl. (cf. Ex. 153).

* *Pan Voyevoda* 67—2 Vns + 2 Ob.; 2 Violas + 2 Cl.

* *Legend of Kitesh* 306—Bass cl. + C-fag. (cf. Ex. 10).

""" 309—Vn. + Fl.

* No. 229. *The Golden Cockerel* 179—Vn. + Picc.; 'Cello + Bass cl.

* As shown in Chap. II, 2 Vns soli or Violin solo + Fl. (Picc.) are often sufficient to double a melody in the upper register.

Examples:

Sadko 207—cf. Chap. II, p. 42 and Ex. 24.

* No. 230. *Russian Easter Fête*, p. 32—2 Solo violins (in harmonics).

* No. 231. *Legend of Kitesh* 297—2 Solo violins + Picc.

Limits of orchestral range.

It is seldom that the entire orchestral conception is centred in the upper register of the orchestra (the 5th and 6th octaves), still more rarely is it focussed wholly in the lowest range (octaves 1 and -1) where the proximity of harmonic intervals creates a bad effect. In the first case the flutes and piccolo should be used along with the upper notes of the violins, *soli* or *divisi*; in the second-107- case the double bassoon and the low notes of the bassoons, bass clarinet, horns, trombones and tuba are brought into play. The first method gives brilliant colour, the second combination is dark and gloomy. The contrary would be fundamentally impossible.

Examples:

Pan Voyevoda 122, 137
Servilia 168, 8th bar. (cf. Ex. 62) } low register.
No. 232. *The Golden Cockerel* 220; cf. also 218, 219

* *Snegourotchka*, before 25

* *Legend of Kitesh*, before 34 } high register.

* No. 233. *The Golden Cockerel* 113, 117

* No. 234. *Shéhérazade*, 2nd movement pp. 59-62

The upper and lower parts of a passage can seldom be widely separated without the intermediate octaves being filled in, for this is contrary to the first principles of proper distribution of chords. Nevertheless the unusual resonance thus produced serves for strange and grotesque effects. In the first of the following examples the piccolo figure doubled by the harp and the sparkling notes of the *glockenspiel* is set about four octaves apart from the bass, which is assigned to a single Double bass and Tuba. But in the 3rd octave, the augmented fourths and diminished fifths in the two flutes help to fill up the intermediate space and lessen the distance between the two extreme parts, thus forming some sort of link between them. The general effect is fanciful.

Examples:

No. 235. *Snegourotchka* 255.

* No. 236. " 315, 5th and 6th bars.

" 274 (cf. Ex. 9).

A Fairy Tale A.

The Golden Cockerel 179, 9th bar. (cf. Ex. 229).

Transference of passages and phrases.

A phrase or a figure is often transferred from one instrument to another. In order to connect the phrases on each instrument in -108- the best possible way, the last note of each part is made to coincide with the first note of the following one. This method is used for passages the range of which is too wide to be performed on any one instrument, or when it is desired to divide a phrase into two different timbres.

Examples:

* *Snegourotchka* 137—The melody is transferred from the violins to the flute and clarinet (cf. Ex. 28).

* " before 191—Solo violin—Solo 'cello.

Pan Voyevoda 57—Trombones—Trumpets; Horn—Ob. + Cl.

A similar operation is used in scoring passages covering the entire orchestral scale, or a great portion of it. When one instrument is on the point of completing its allotted part, another instrument takes up the passage, starting on one or two notes common to both parts, and so on. This division must be carried out to ensure the balance of the whole passage.

Examples:

Snegourotchka 36, 38, 131—Strings.

The Tsar's Bride 190—Wood-wind.

Sadko 72—Strings (cf. Ex. 112).

" 223—Strings.

The Christmas Night, before 180—Strings, wind and chorus (cf. Ex. 132).

* No. 237. *The Christmas Night*, before 181—String figure.

* *Servilia* 111—Strings (cf. Ex. 88).

" 29, 5th bar.—Ob.—Fl.; Cl.—Bass cl., Fag.

No. 238. *The Golden Cockerel*, before 9—Wood-wind.

* """ 5—Fag.—Eng. horn (+ 'Cellos *pizz.*).

Chords of different tone quality used alternately.

1. The most usual practice is to employ chords on different groups of instruments alternately. In dealing with chords in different registers care should be taken that the progression of parts, though broken in passing from one group to another, remains as regular-109- as if there were no leap from octave to octave; this applies specially to chromatic passages in order to avoid false relation.

Examples:

No. 239. *Ivan the Terrible*, Act II 29.

No. 240-241. *The Tsar's Bride* 123, before 124.

* No. 242-243. """ 178, 179.

* *Note.* The rules regulating progression of parts may sometimes be ignored, when extreme contrast of timbre between two adjacent chords is intended.

Examples:

* *Shéhérazade*, 8th bar from the beginning, (the chromatic progression at the 12th bar is undertaken by the same instruments, the 2nd cl. is therefore placed above the first in the opening)—cf. Ex. 109.

* *The Christmas Night*, opening (cf. Ex. 106).

2. Another excellent method consists in transferring *the same chord or its inversion* from one orchestral group to another. This operation demands perfect balance in progression of parts as well as register. The first group strikes a chord of short value, the other group takes possession of it simultaneously in the same position and distribution, either in the same octave or in another. The dynamic gradations of tone need not necessarily be the same in both groups.

Examples:

Ivan the Terrible, commencement of the overture (cf. Ex. 85).

No. 244. *Snegourotchka* 140.

Amplification and elimination of tone qualities.

The operation which consists in contrasting the resonance of two different groups (* or the different timbres of one and the same group), either in sustained notes or chords, transforms a simple into a complex timbre, suddenly, or by degrees. It is used in establishing a *crescendo*. While the first group effects the *crescendo* gradually, the second group enters *piano* or *pianissimo*, and attains its *crescendo* more rapidly. The whole process is thereby rendered more tense as the timbre changes. The converse operation—the transition from a complex to a simple timbre, by the suppression of one of the groups, belongs essentially to the *diminuendo*.-110-

Examples:

No. 245. *Snegourotchka* 313.

" 140 (cf. Ex. 244).

A Fairy Tale V.

Shéhérazade, 2nd movement D (cf. Ex. 74).

* " 4th movement p. 221.

No. 246. *Servilia* 228; cf. also 44.

The Christmas Night 165 (cf. Ex. 143).

No. 247. *The Tsar's Bride*, before 205.

* No. 248. *Russian Easter Fête* D.

* No. 249-250. *Legend of Kitesh* 5, 162.

Repetition of phrases, imitation, echo.

As regards choice of timbre, phrases in imitation are subject to the law of register. When a phrase is imitated in the upper register it should be given to an instrument of higher range and *vice versa*. If this rule is ignored an unnatural effect will be produced, as when the clarinet in its upper range replies to the oboe in the lower compass etc. The same rule must be followed in dealing with phrases, actually different, but similar in character; repeated phrases of different character should be scored in a manner most suitable to each.

Examples:

The Tsar's Bride 157, 161.

Legend of Kitesh 40-41.

* No. 251. *Spanish Capriccio* S.

In echo phrases, that is to say imitation entailing not only decrease in volume of tone but also an effect of distance, the second instrument should be weaker than the first, but the two should possess some sort of affinity. An echo given to muted brass following the same phrase not muted produces this distant effect. Muted trumpets are eminently suited to echo a theme in the oboes; flutes also may imitate clarinets and oboes successfully. A wood-wind instrument cannot be used to echo the strings, or-111- *vice versa*, on account of the dissimilarity in timbre. Imitation in octaves (with a decrease in resonance) creates an effect resembling an echo.

Examples:

Ivan the Terrible, Act III 3.

No. 252. *Sadko* 264.

* *Spanish Capriccio* E.—This example is not precisely an echo but resembles one in character (cf. Ex. 44).

* *Shéhérazade*, 4th movement before O.

Sforzando-piano and *piano-sforzando* chords.

Besides the natural dynamic process of obtaining these marks of expression, a process which depends upon the player, they may also be produced by artificial means of orchestration.

a) At the moment when the wood-wind begins a *piano* chord, the strings attack it *sforzando*, a compound chord for preference, either *arco* or *pizz*. In the opposite case the *sf* in the strings must occur at the end of the wood-wind chord. The first method is also employed for a *sf-dim.*, and the second for a *cresc.-sf* effect.

b) It is not so effective, and therefore less frequent to give the notes of sustained value to the strings, and the short chords to the wood-wind. In such cases the *tenuto* chord is played *tremolando* on the strings.

Examples:

Vera Scheloga, before 35, 38, 10th bar.

* No. 253. *Legend of Kitesh*, before 15-16.

* *Shéhérazade*, 2nd movement, P, 14th bar.

Method of emphasising certain notes and chords.

In order to stress or emphasise a certain note or chord, besides the marks of expression ⟫ and *sf*, chords of 2, 3, and 4 notes can be inserted into the melodic progression by the instruments of the string quartet, each playing a single note; short notes in the wood-wind may also be used as well as a chain of three or -112- four grace notes, in the form of a scale, either in strings or wood-wind. These unstressed notes (anacrusis), generally written very small, form a kind of upward glide, the downward direction being less common. As a rule they are connected to the main note by a slur. In the strings they should not lead up to chords of three or four notes, as this would be awkward for the bow.

Examples:

No. 254. *The Tsar's Bride* 142—Anacrusis in the strings.

* No. 255. *Shéhérazade*, 2nd movement C—Short *pizz.* chords.

* """ P—Short wind chords (cf. Ex. 19).

Crescendo and *diminuendo*.

Short *crescendi* and *diminuendi* are generally produced by natural dynamic means; when prolonged, they are obtained by this method combined with other orchestral devices. After the strings, the brass is the group most facile in producing dynamic shades of expression, glorifying *crescendo* chords into the most brilliant *sforzando* climaxes. Clarinets specialise in *diminuendo* effects and are capable of decreasing their tone to a breath (*morendo*). Prolonged orchestral *crescendi* are obtained by the gradual addition of other instruments in the following order: strings, wood-wind, brass. *Diminuendo* effects are accomplished by the elimination of the instruments in the reverse order (brass, wood-wind, strings). The scope of this work does not lend itself to the quotation of prolonged *crescendo* and *diminuendo* passages. The reader is referred, therefore, to the full scores:

* *Shéhérazade*, pp. 5-7, 92-96, 192-200.

* *Antar* 6, 51.

* *The Christmas Night* 183.

* *Sadko* 165-166.

* *The Tsar's Bride* 80-81.

Many examples of shorter *crescendi* and *diminuendi* will be found in Vol. II.-113-

Diverging and converging progressions.

In the majority of cases, diverging and converging progressions simply consist in the gradual ascent of the three upper parts, with the bass descending. The distance separating the bass from the other parts is trifling at first, and grows by degrees. On the other hand, in converging progressions, the three upper parts, at first so far distant from the bass, gradually approach it. Sometimes these progressions involve an increase or a decrease in tone. The intermediate intervals are filled up by the introduction of fresh parts as the distance widens, so that the upper parts become doubled or trebled. In converging progressions the tripled and doubled parts are simplified, as the duplicating instruments cease to play. Moreover, if the harmony allows it, the group in the middle region which remains stationary is the group to be retained, or else the sustained note which guarantees unity in the operation. Below, the reader will find double examples of both descriptions. The first pair represents a diverging progression, 1. *piano*, in which the human voice takes part; 2. a purely orchestral *crescendo*. The second depicts two similar diverging progressions, firstly a gradual *crescendo*, secondly *dim.*, during which the strings become more and more divided as the wind instruments cease to play. Ex. 258 accompanies the apparition of Mlada, Ex. 259, its disappearance. The atmosphere and colouring are weird and fanciful. The third pair of examples forms instances of converging progressions. In the first (Ex. 260) Princess Volkhova relates the wonders of the sea. Then in the middle of a powerful orchestral *crescendo* the Sea-King appears (Ex. 261). Both examples include a sustained stationary chord of the diminished seventh. The handling of such progressions requires the greatest care.

Examples:

No. 256-257. *The Tsar's Bride* 102 and 107.

No. 258-259. *Mlada*, Act III 12 and 19.

No. 260-261. *Sadko* 105 and 119.

Sadko 72 (cf. Ex. 112).

" before 315.

-114-

* *The Christmas Night*, beginning (cf. Ex. 106).

* No. 262. *Antar*, end of 3rd movement.

Note. A sustained note between the diverging parts does not always allow the empty space to be more completely filled up.

Example:

No. 263. *The Golden Cockerel*, before 106.

Tone quality as a harmonic force.

Harmonic basis.

Melodic design comprising notes foreign to the harmony, passing or grace notes, embellishments etc., does not permit that a florid outline should proceed at the same time with another one, reduced to essential and fundamental notes:

Melodic design.

Fundamental notes.

[Listen]

If, in the above example, the upper part is transposed an octave lower, the discordant effect produced by the contact of appoggiaturas and fundamental notes will be diminished; the quicker the passage is played the less harsh the effect will be, and *vice versa*. But it would be ill-advised to lay down any hard and fast rule as to the permissible length of these notes. There is no doubt that the harmonic notes, the thirds of the fundamental one (*E*) are more prominent from their proximity with the notes extraneous to the harmony. If the number of parts is increased (for instance, if the melodic figure is in thirds, sixths etc.), the question becomes still more complicated, since, to the original harmonic scheme, chords with different root bases are added, producing false relation.

Nevertheless, for the solution of such problems, orchestration provides an element of the greatest importance: difference of timbres. The greater the dissimilarity in timbre between the harmonic basis on the one hand and the melodic design on the other, the less discordant the notes extraneous to the harmony-115- will sound. The best example of this is to be found between the human voice and the orchestra, next comes the difference of timbres between the groups of strings, wood-wind, plucked strings and percussion instruments. Less important differences occur between wood-wind and brass; in these two groups, therefore, the harmonic basis generally remains an octave removed from the melodic design, and should be of inferior dynamic power.

Examples of harmonic basis in chords:

No. 264. *Pan Voyevoda*, Introduction.

Legend of Kitesh, Introduction (cf. also Ex. 125 and 140).

* *Mlada*, Act III 10.

The harmonic basis may be ornamental in character, in which case it should move independently of the concurrent melodic design.

Examples:

* No. 265-266. *Tsar Saltan* 103-104, 128, 149, 162-165 (cf. below).

Chords the most widely opposed in character may be used on a simple, stationary harmonic basis, a basis, founded, for example, on the chord of the tonic or diminished seventh.

Examples:

No. 267. *Legend of Kitesh* 326-328—Wood-wind and harps on a string basis.

No. 268-269. *Kashtcheï the Immortal* 33, 43.

No. 270. *Mlada*, Act II, before 17, 18], 20.

No. 271. *The Golden Cockerel* 125—Chords of the diminished seventh, on arpeggio basis (augmented fifth).

The effect of alternating harmony produced between two melodic figures, e.g. one transmitting a note, held in abeyance, to the other, or the simultaneous progression of a figure in augmentation and diminution etc. becomes comprehensible and pleasant to the ear when the fundamental sustained harmony is different.-116-

Examples:

Legend of Kitesh 34, 36, 297 (cf. Ex. 34 and 231).

No. 272-274. *Tsar Saltan* 104, 162-165 (cf. also 147-148).

* *Russian Easter Fête*, before V.

The whole question as to what is allowed and what forbidden in the employment of notes extraneous to the harmony is one of the most difficult in the whole range of composition; the permissible length of such notes is in no way established. In absence of artistic feeling, the composer who relies entirely on the difference between two timbres will often find himself using the most painful discords. Innovations in this direction in the latest post-Wagnerian music are often very questionable; they depress the ear and deaden the musical senses, leading to the unnatural conclusion that what is good, taken separately, must necessarily be good in combination.

Artificial effects.

I apply this name to some orchestral operations which are based on certain defects of hearing and faculty of perception. Having no wish to specify those that already exist or to foretell those which may yet be invented, I will mention, in passing, a few which have been used by me in my own works. To this class belong *glissando* scales or arpeggios in the harp, the notes of which do not correspond with those played simultaneously by other instruments, but which are used from the fact that long *glissandi* are more resonant and brilliant than short ones.

Examples:

Snegourotchka 325 (cf. Ex. 95).

No. 275. *Pan Voyevoda* 128.

* *Shéhérazade*, 3rd movement M, 5th bar (cf. Ex. 248).

* *Russian Easter Fête* D (cf. Ex. 248).

* Enharmonic *glissando* in the strings should also be mentioned.

No. 276. *The Christmas Night* 180, 13th bar—'Cellos *glissando*.-117-

Use of percussion instruments for rhythm and colour.

Whenever some portion of the orchestra executes a rhythmic figure, percussion instruments should always be employed concurrently. An insignificant and playful rhythm is suitable to the triangle, tambourine, castanets and side drum, a vigourous and straightforward rhythm may be given to the bass drum, cymbals and gong. The strokes on these instruments should almost invariably correspond to the strong beats of the bar, highly-accented syncopated notes or disconnected *sforzandi*. The triangle, side drum and tambourine are capable of various rhythmic figures. Sometimes the percussion is used separately, independently of any other group of instruments.

The brass and wood-wind are the two groups which combine the most satisfactorily with percussion from the standpoint of colour. The triangle, side drum, and tambourine go best with harmony in the upper register; cymbals, bass drum and gong with harmony in the lower. The following are the combinations most generally employed: *tremolo* on the triangle and tambourine with trills in wood-wind and violins; *tremolo* on the side drum, or cymbals struck with drum sticks, and sustained chords on trumpets and horns; *tremolo* on the bass drum or the gong with chords on trombones or low sustained notes on 'cellos and double basses. It must not be forgotten that the bass drum, cymbals, gong and a *tremolo* on the side drum, played *fortissimo*, is sufficient to overpower any orchestral *tutti*.

* The reader will find instances of the use of percussion instruments in any full score, and in several examples of the present work.

Examples:

* *Shéhérazade* pp. 107-119, also many passages in 4th movement.

* *Antar* 40, 43 (cf. Ex. 73, 29).

* *Spanish capriccio* P (cf. Ex. 64); the cadences to be studied in the 4th movement, where they are accompanied by various percussion instruments.

* *Russian Easter Fête* K (cf. Ex. 217).

* *The Tsar's Bride* 140.

* *Legend of Kitesh* 196-197—"The Battle of Kerjémetz".

* *Pan Voyevoda* 71-72.-118-

Economy in orchestral colour.

Neither musical feeling nor the ear itself can stand, for long, the full resources of the orchestra combined together. The favourite group of instruments is the strings, then follow in order the wood-wind, brass, kettle-drums, harps, *pizzicato* effects, and lastly the percussion, also, in point of order, triangle, cymbals, big drum, side drum, tambourine, gong. Further removed stand the celesta, *glockenspiel* and xylophone, which instruments, though melodic, are too characteristic in timbre to be employed over frequently. The same may be said of the piano and castanets. A quantity of national instruments not included in the present work may be incorporated into the orchestra; such are the guitar, the domra, zither, mandoline, the oriental tambourine, small tambourine etc. These instruments are employed from time to time for descriptive-aesthetic purposes.

These instruments are most frequently used in the above-named order. A group of instruments which has been silent for some time gains fresh interest upon its reappearance. The trombones, trumpets and tuba are occasionally *tacet* for long periods, the percussion is seldom employed, and practically never all together, but in single instruments or in two's and three's. In national dances or music in ballad style, percussion instruments may be used more freely.

After a long rest the re-entry of the horns, trombones and tuba should coincide with some characteristic intensity of tone, either *pp* or *ff*; *piano* and *forte* re-entries are less successful, while re-introducing these instruments *mezzo-forte* or *mezzo-piano* produces a colourless and common-place effect. This remark is capable of wider application. For the same reasons it is not good to commence or finish any piece of music either *mf* or *mp*. The scope of the musical examples in this work does not permit of illustrating by quotation the use of economy in orchestral colour, nor the re-entry of instruments thrown into prominence by prolonged rests. The reader must examine these questions in full scores.

Chapter V.

COMBINATION OF THE HUMAN VOICE WITH ORCHESTRA.
THE STAGE BAND.

Orchestral accompaniment of solo voices.

General remarks.

In accompanying the voice orchestral scoring should be light enough for the singer to make free use of all the dynamic shades of expression without hardness of tone. In overflowing lyrical moments, where full voice is required, the singer should be well supported by the orchestra.

Opera singing may be divided into two general classes, lyric singing and declamation or recitative. The full, round, *legato* aria affords greater facility for tone production than florid music or recitative, and the more movement and rhythmic detail contained in the vocal part, the greater freedom and liberty must there be given to the voice. In such a case the latter should not be doubled by the orchestra, neither should rhythmical figures be written for any instrument corresponding with those in the vocal part. In accompanying the voice the composer should bear these points in mind before turning his attention to the choice of orchestral colour. A confused, heavy accompaniment will overpower the singer; an accompaniment which is too simple in character will lack interest, and one which is too weak will not sustain the voice sufficiently.

In modern opera it is rare that orchestral writing is confined to accompaniment pure and simple. It frequently happens that the principal musical idea, often complex in character, is contained in the orchestra. The voice may then be said to form the accompaniment, exchanging musical for literary interest. It becomes-120- subordinate to the orchestra, as though it were an extra part, subsequently added as an after-thought. But it is evident that great care must be taken with orchestral writing in such cases. The scoring must not be so heavy or complicated as to drown the voice and prevent the words from being heard, thereby breaking the thread of the text, and leaving the musical imagery unexplained. Certain moments may require great volume of orchestral tone, so great that a voice of even phenomenal power is incapable of being heard. Even if the singer is audible, such unequal struggles between voice and orchestra are most inartistic, and the composer should reserve his orchestral outbursts for the intervals during which the voice is silent, distributing the singer's phrases and pauses in a free and natural manner, according to the sense of the words. If a prolonged *forte* passage occurs in the orchestra it may be used concurrently with action on the stage. All artificial reduction of tone contrary to the true feeling of a passage, the sole object being to allow the voice to come through, should be strictly avoided, as it deprives orchestral writing of its distinctive brilliance. It must also be remembered that too great a disparity in volume of tone between purely orchestral passages and those which accompany the voice create an inartistic comparison. Therefore, when the orchestra is strengthened by the use of wood-wind in three's or four's, and brass in large numbers, the division of tone and colour must be manipulated skillfully and with the greatest care.

In previous sections I have frequently stated that the structure of the orchestra is closely related to the music itself. The scoring of a vocal work proves this relationship in a striking manner, and, indeed, it may be stipulated that *only that which is well written can be well orchestrated.*

Transparence of accompaniment. Harmony.

The group of strings is the most transparent medium and the one least likely to overpower the voice. Then come the wood-wind and the brass, the latter in the following order: horns, trombones, trumpets. A combination of strings, *pizz.*, and the harp forms a setting eminently favourable for the voice. As a general rule a singer is more easily overpowered by long sustained notes than by short detached ones. Strings doubled in the wood-wind and brass, and brass doubled by wood-wind are combinations liable to drown the singer. This may be done even more easily by *tremolando* in the kettle-drums and other percussion instruments, which, even by themselves are capable of overpowering any other orchestral group of instruments. Doubling of wood-wind and horns, and the use of two clarinets, two oboes or two horns in unison to form one harmonic part is likewise to be avoided, as such combinations will have a similar effect on the voice. The frequent use of long sustained notes in the double basses is another course unfavourable to the singer; these notes in combination with the human voice produce a peculiar throbbing effect.

Juxtaposition of strings and wood-wind which overweights *legato* or declamatory singing may nevertheless be employed if one of the groups forms the harmony in sustained notes and the other executes a melodic design, when, for instance the sustaining instruments are clarinet, and bassoon, or bassoon and horn, and the melodic design is entrusted to violins or violas—or in the opposite case, when the harmony is given to violas and 'cellos *divisi*, and the harmonic figure to the clarinets.

Sustained harmony in the register of the second octave to the middle of the third does not overpower women's voices, as these develop *outside* this range; neither is it too heavy for men's voices, which although opening out *within* the range itself sound an octave higher, as in the case of the tenor voice. As a rule women's voices suffer more than men's when they come in contact with harmony in a register similar to their own. Taken separately, and used in moderation, each group of orchestral instruments may be considered favourable to each type of voice. But the combination of two or three groups cannot be so considered unless they each play an independent part and are not united together at full strength. Incessant four-part harmony is to be deprecated. Satisfactory results will be obtained when the number of harmonic parts is gradually decreased, with some of them sustaining pedal notes, and when the harmony, interspersed with necessary pauses is confined to the limits of one octave, distributed over several octaves, or duplicated in the higher register.

These manipulations allow the composer to come to the singer's aid; in voice-modulations, when the singer passes from the *can-122-tabile* to the declamatory style, the composer may reduce or eliminate some harmony which is found to be too heavy as the vocal tone diminishes, and conversely, support the voice by a fuller orchestral tone in broad phrases and climaxes.

Ornamental writing and polyphonic accompaniment should never be too intricate in character, entailing the use of an unnecessary number of instruments. Some complicated figures are better partially entrusted to *pizz.* strings and harp, as this combination has little chance of overpowering the voice. Some examples of accompanying an *aria* are given below.

Examples:

The Tsar's Bride, Lykow's supplementary *Aria* (Act III).

""" 16-19—Griasnov's *Aria*.

No. 277. *Snegourotchka* 45.

* *Snegourotchka* 187-188, 212-213 the two Cavatinas of Tsar Berendey (cf. extracts, Ex. 102, 225).

No. 278. *Sadko* 143.

" 204-206—The Venetian's Song.

* *Legend of Kitesh* 39-41, 222-223 (cf. Ex. 31).

* *The Golden Cockerel* 153-157, 163.

Florid singing which limits volume of tone requires a light accompaniment, simple in outline and colour, involving no duplication of instruments.

Examples:

No. 279. *Snegourotchka* 42-48—*Snegourotchka's Aria* (Prologue), Fragment.

* *Sadko* 195-197—Hindoo Song (cf. Ex. 122).

* *The Christmas Night* 45-50—Oxana's *Aria*.

* *The Golden Cockerel* 131-136—*Aria* of Queen Shémakhâ.

Doubling voices in the orchestra.

Melodic doubling of voices by orchestral instruments (in unison or octaves) is of frequent occurrence, but incessant duplication for an extended period of time should be avoided; it is only permissible in isolated phrases. The most natural duplication in-123- unison of womens' voices is performed by violins, violas, clarinets and oboes; that of mens' voices by violas, 'cellos, bassoons and horns. Doubling in octaves is usually done in the upper register. Trombones and trumpets overpower the voice and cannot be used for this purpose. Uninterrupted or too frequent duplication should be avoided, not only because the operation deprives the singer of full freedom of expression, but also because it replaces by a mixed timbre the rare characteristic qualities of the human voice. Doubling, when limited to a few special phrases supports the voice and endows it with beauty and colour. It is only suitable *in tempo*; to apply it, in unison or octaves to a passage *ad. lib.* is both ineffective and dangerous.

Examples:

Snegourotchka 50-52—Snegourotchka's Arietta (cf. Ex. 41).

Sadko 309-311—Volkhova's Cradle-song (cf. Ex. 81).

Besides the question of doubling the voice for the object of colour there are instances when the singer executes only part of a phrase, allotted in its entirely to an orchestral instrument.

Example:

Vera Scheloga 30, 36 (cf. Ex. 49).

Lyrical climaxes, *a piena voce*, or dramatic passages for the voice situated outside its normal range should be supported melodically and harmonically by the orchestra, in the register in which the voice is placed. The culminating point in such passages often coincides with the entry or sudden attack of the trombones or other brass instruments, or by a rush of strings. Strengthening the accompaniment in this manner will soften the tone of the voice.

Examples:

No. 280. *The Tsar's Bride* 206.

Servilia 126-127.

" 232.

No. 281. *Sadko* 314.

Vera Scheloga 41.-124-

If the culminating point is soft in colour and outline it is better left unsupported in the orchestra, but sometimes the wood-wind, sustaining such passages with light transparent melody or harmony may produce an entrancing effect.

Examples:

Snegourotchka 188.

" 318 (cf. Ex. 119).

No. 282. *The Tsar's Bride* 214.

It is a common practice to support voices in concerted numbers by harmony and duplication; this operation makes for accuracy and brilliance when applied to duets, trios, quartets etc.

Examples:

Snegourotchka 292-293—Duet (cf. Ex. 118).

Sadko 99-101—Duet (cf. Ex. 289 and 290).

No. 283. *The Tsar's Bride* 169—sextet.

""" 117 quartet.

Legend of Kitesh 341—quartet and sextet (cf. Ex. 305).

The beautiful effect produced by a solo instrument accompanying a *cantabile aria* cannot be denied. In such cases the instruments used are generally the violin, viola, and 'cello, or the flute, oboe, Eng. horn, clar., bass clar., bassoon, horn and harp. The accompaniment is often contrapuntal or composed of polyphonic designs. The solo instrument either plays alone or as the leading melodic voice in the *ensemble*. In combination with the voice, or associated with some action on the stage, a solo instrument is a powerful expedient for musical characterisation. Instances of this description are numerous.

Examples:

Snegourotchka 50—Soprano and oboe (cf. Ex. 41).

" 97—Contralto and Eng. horn.

" 243, 246—Baritone and bass clar. (cf. Ex. 47-48).

No. 284. *The Tsar's Bride* 108—Soprano, 'cello and oboe.

* *The Golden Cockerel* 163—Soprano and viola (cf. Ex. 226).-125-

It is comparatively rare for percussion instruments to take part in accompanying the voice. The triangle is occasionally used, the cymbals less frequently. An accompaniment may be formed by a figure or a *tremolo* on the kettle-drums.

Examples:

Snegourotchka 97, 224, 247 (Lell's 1st and 3rd songs).

Tsar Saltan, before 5.

* No. 285. *The Golden Cockerel* 135; cf. also 161, 197.

The following are examples of powerful and expressive orchestral passages, the voice *tacet*:

No. 286. *The Tsar's Bride* 81.

* *Legend of Kitesh* 282, 298.

* *Servilia* 130.

Recitative and declamation.

The accompaniment of recitative and melodic declamatory phrases should be light enough to allow the voice to come through without strain, and the words to be heard distinctly. The most convenient method is to employ sustained chords and *tremolo* on the strings or wood-wind, giving free latitude to the voice from a rhythmic point of view (*a piacere*).

Another excellent plan is to write short chords in the strings combined with wood-wind in different ways. Sustained chords and those entailing change of position should occur preferably when the voice is silent, thus permitting both conductor and orchestra to keep a closer watch over the singer's irregularities of rhythm in *a piacere* recitatives. If the accompaniment is more complex in character, melodic, polyphonic or ornamental in design, the recitative must be sung *in tempo*. Any phrase which it is necessary to emphasise in accordance with the sense of the words assumes a more *cantabile* character, and must be reinforced by the orchestra. Opera, today, besides demanding much greater care in the treatment of the text than in the past, abounds in constant transition from declamation to *cantabile*, or in the fusion of the two. The orchestra offers more variety of texture and must be-126- handled with greater regard to its relationship to the words, and the action on the stage. This class of orchestration can only be studied from lengthy examples. I refer the reader to operatic full scores and content myself with giving one or short instances:

Examples:

No. 287. *Snegourotchka* 16.

No. 288. *The Tsar's Bride* 124-125.

The following double examples, similar from a musical point of view, show different methods of handling an orchestra from the standpoint of accompaniment to the voice, and the *tutti* form.

Examples:

No. 289-291. *Sadko* 99-101 and 305-307 (compare also Ex. 75).

Vera Scheloga 3-7 and 28.

Care should be taken not to score too heavily when accompanying singers in the wings.

Examples:

* No. 292. *Sadko* 316, 318, 320.

* *Legend of Kitesh* 286-289, 304-305.

Orchestral accompaniment of the chorus.

The chorus, possessing much greater unity and power than the solo voice, does not demand such careful handling in the accompaniment. On the contrary, too great a refinement of orchestral treatment will prove harmful to the resonance of the chorus. As a general rule orchestration of choral works follows the rules laid down for purely instrumental scoring. It is obvious that dynamic marks of expression must correspond in both bodies, but doubling one orchestral group with another and coupling instruments of the same kind in unison (2 Ob., 2 Cl., 4 Horns, 3 Trombones etc.) are both possible operations, if performed according to the requirements of the musical context. Doubling choral parts by instruments is generally a good plan. In *cantabile* passages such-127- duplication may be melodic in character, and the design more ornamental in the orchestra than in the chorus.

Examples:

Ivan the Terrible, Act II 3-6; Act III 66-69.

The May Night, Act I X-Y; Act III L-Ee, Ddd-Fff.

Snegourotchka 61-73, 147-153, 323-328.

Mlada, Act II 22-31, 45-63; Act IV 31-36.

The Christmas Night 59-61, 115-123.

Sadko 37-39, 50-53, 79-86, 173, 177, 187, 189, 218-221, 233, 270-273.

The Tsar's Bride 29-30, 40-42, 50-59, 141.

Tsar Saltan 67-71, 91-93, 133-145, 207-208.

Legend of Kitesh 167, 177-178.

The Golden Cockerel 237-238, 262-264.

The reader will find instances of choral accompaniment in many examples relating to other sections of the work.

In the case of solitary exclamations or phrases in recitative, melodic doubling is not always suitable. It is better to support the voice simply by harmonic duplication.

The repetition of notes—required by declamation—forming no fundamental part of the rhythmical structure of a phrase or chord should not be reproduced in the orchestra; the melodic or harmonic basis alone should be doubled. Sometimes the rhythmical structure of a choral phrase is simplified in comparison with its orchestral duplication.

Examples:

No. 293. *The Tsar's Bride* 96.

No. 294. *Ivan the Terrible*, Act I, before 75.

Choral passages, the musical context of which is complete in itself, forming a chorus *a cappella* often remain undoubled by the orchestra, accompanied solely by sustained notes or an independent polyphonic figure.-128-

Examples:

No. 295. *Sadko* 219.

* *Tsar Saltan* 207.

* *Legend of Kitesh* 167 (cf. Ex. 116).

* *The Golden Cockerel* 236.

Heavier scoring is required for a mixed chorus; for a male voice chorus the orchestration should be lighter; still more so for women's voices alone. In scoring a certain passage the composer should not lose sight of the number of choristers he is employing, for scenic conditions may necessitate a reduction of that figure. The approximate number should be marked in the full score as a basis upon which to work.

Examples:

No. 296. *Ivan the Terrible*, Act II 37.

* *Sadko* 17, 20.

* *Legend of Kitesh* 61 (cf. Ex. 198).

Note. It must also be remembered that a *ff* passage on an d orchestra, comprising wood-wind in fours, and numerous brass (sometimes in three's), is capable of overpowering a large mixed chorus.

A chorus in the wings requires as light an accompaniment as that employed for a solo singer on the stage.

Examples:

* *Ivan the Terrible*, Act I 25-26, 90; Act III 13-14.

* *The May Night*, Act I, before X; Act III Bbb-Ccc.

* No. 297. *Sadko* 102.

* *Legend of Kitesh* 54-56 (cf. Ex. 196 and 197).

Solo voice with chorus.

When an *aria* or recitative is coupled with the chorus great care must be taken in the choral writing. A woman's solo voice stands out well against a male voice chorus, likewise a solo male voice against a women's chorus, for in both cases, the timbre of the solo voice differs from the rest. But the combination of solo-129- voice and chorus, of the same timbre, or mixed chorus, creates a certain amount of difficulty. In such cases the soloist should sing in a higher register than the chorus, the former *a piena voce*, the latter *piano*. The soloist should stand as near to the footlights as possible; the chorus up-stage. The orchestration should be adapted to the soloist, not to the chorus.

Examples:

No. 298. *Snegourotchka* 143.

Ivan the Terrible. Act II 37 (cf. Ex. 296).

When the chorus sings in the wings the soloist is always heard distinctly.

Examples:

Ivan the Terrible, Act I 25-26.

* *The May Night*, Act III Ccc.

* *Sadko* 102, 111.

Instruments on the stage and in the wings.

The use of instruments on the stage or in the wings dates from distant times (Mozart, *Don Giovanni*, string orchestra in Act I, *finale*). In the middle of last century orchestras of brass instruments, or brass and wood-wind combined, made their appearance on the stage (Glinka, Meyerbeer, Gounod and others). More modern composers have abandoned this clumsy practice, not only unfortunate from the spectators' point of view, but also detrimental to the mediaeval or legendary setting of the majority of operas. Only those stage instruments are now used which suit the scene and surroundings in which the opera is laid. As regards instruments in the wings, invisible to the audience, the question is simple. Nevertheless, for the musician of today the choice of these instruments must be regulated by aesthetic considerations of greater importance than those governing the selection of a military band. The instruments are played in the wings, those visible on the stage are only for ornament. Sometimes stage-instruments may be replicas of those common to the period which the opera represents, (the sacred horns in *Mlada*, for example). The orchestral accompaniment-130- must vary in power according to the characteristics of the instruments played in the wings. It is impossible to illustrate the use of all the instruments mentioned below, and to outline suitable accompaniments. I can only give a few examples and refer the reader once again to the passages in the full scores.

a) Trumpets:

Servilia 12, 25.

* *Legend of Kitesh* 53, 55, 60.

* *Tsar Saltan* 139 and further on.

b) Horns, in the form of hunting horns:

Pan Voyevoda 38-39.

c) Trombones, leaving the orchestra to go on the stage:

Pan Voyevoda 191.

d) Cornets:

Ivan the Terrible, Act III 3, 7.

e) Sacred horns (natural brass instruments in various keys):

Mlada, Act II, pp. 179 onwards.

f) Small clarinets and piccolos:

No. 299-300. *Mlada*, Act III 37, 39.

g) Pipes of Pan: instruments, specially made, with many holes which are passed over the lips. These particular pipes produce a special enharmonic scale (*B* flat, *C*, *D* flat, *E* flat, *E*, *F* sharp, *G*, *A*), which has the effect of a glissando:

Mlada, Act III 39, 43 (cf. Ex. 300).

h) Harp, reproducing the effect of an aeolian harp:

Kashtcheï the Immortal 32 and further on (cf. Ex. 268, 269).

i) Lyres. Instruments specially made and tuned so as to be able to perform a glissando chord of the diminished seventh:

Mlada, Act III 39, 43 (cf. Ex. 300).

k) Pianoforte, grand or upright:

Mozart and Salieri 22-23.

l) Gong, imitating a church bell:

Ivan the Terrible, Act I 57 and further on.-131-

m) Bass Drum (without cymbals) to imitate the sound of cannon:

Tsar Saltan 139 and later.

n) Small kettle-drum, in *D* flat (3rd octave):

Mlada, Act III 41 and later (cf. Ex. 60).

o) Bells in various keys:

Sadko 128 and 139.

No. 301. *Legend of Kitesh* 181 and further on. See also 241, 323 and later.

* *Tsar Saltan* 139 and further on.

p) Organ:

No. 302. *Sadko* 299-300.

Wood-wind and strings are comparatively seldom used on the stage or in the wings. In Russian opera the strings are employed in this way by Rubinstein (*Gorioucha*), and in a splendidly characteristic manner by Serov (*Hostile Power*): in the latter opera the *E* flat clarinet is used to imitate the fife in the Carnival procession.[17]

Chapter VI (Supplementary).

VOICES.

Technical Terms.

Among all the confused terms employed in singing to denote the compass, register and character of the human voice, there are four which may be said to represent elemental types: soprano, alto or contralto, tenor and bass. These names are used to denote the composition of the chorus with sub-divisions of *firsts* and *seconds*, to determine how the parts must be divided. (Sopr. I, Sopr. II etc.) While the range of an instrument is exactly governed by its construction, the compass of the voice, on the other hand, depends on the individuality of the singer. It is therefore impossible to define the exact limits of each of these vocal types. When it is a question of dividing choristers into 1st and 2nd parts, those with the higher voices are classed among the firsts and *vice versa*.

Besides the principal terms mentioned above, the names mezzo-soprano (between sop. and alto), and baritone (between tenor and bass) are also employed.

Note. In the chorus mezzo-sopranos are classed with 2nd sopranos or 1st altos, baritones with 2nd tenors or first basses, according to quality and timbre of voice.

Apart from these denominations which represent the six principal solo voices, a quantity of others are in use to denote either compass, timbre or technique, such as light soprano, *soprano giusto*, lyric soprano, dramatic soprano, light tenor, *tenorino-altino*, *baryton-martin*, lyric tenor, dramatic tenor, *basso cantante* ("singing bass"), *basso profondo* (deep bass) etc. To this lengthy list must-133- be added the term *mezzo-carattere*, of intermediate character (between lyric and dramatic soprano, for example).

If we try to discover the real meaning of these designations it soon becomes apparent that they are derived from widely different sources—for instance, "light soprano" implies agility and mobility in the voice; "dramatic tenor", the power to express strong dramatic feeling; *basso profondo* signifies great resonance in the deep register.

Minute examination of all the methods of attack and emission of sound lies within the province of the singing master and to enumerate them here would only perplex the student. The same applies to the position and exact limits of register (chest voice, middle and head voice in women; chest voice, mixed voice and falsetto in men). The work of a teacher of singing consists in equalising the voice throughout its whole compass, so that the transition from one register to another, on all the vowels, may be accomplished imperceptibly. Some voices are naturally even and flexible. The professor of singing must correct faults in breathing, determine the range of the voice and place it, equalise its tone, increase its flexibility, instruct as to the pronunciation of vowels, modulation from one grade of expression to another, etc. A composer should be able to rely upon flexible and equal voices without having to trouble himself as to the abilities or defects of individual singers. In these days a part is seldom written for a particular artist, and composers and librettists do not find it necessary to entrust a certain rôle to *fioriture* singers, another to heavy dramatic voices. Poetic and artistic considerations demand greater variety of resource in the study of opera or vocal music in general.

Soloists.

Range and register.

I advise the composer to be guided by Table F. which gives the approximate range of the six principal solo voices. A bracket under the notes defines the normal octave, the register in which the voice is generally used. Within these limits the composer may write freely without fear of hardening or tiring the voice.-134- The normal octave applies also to declamatory singing and recitative; the notes above it are exceptional and should be used for the culminating points of a passage or for climaxes, the notes below, for the fall or decline of a melody. Employing voices in unusual registers for long periods of time will weary both singer and listener, but these registers may occasionally be used for brief intervals so as not to confine the voice too strictly to one octave. A few examples are added to illustrate melody in different types of voices.

Examples:

The Tsar's Bride 102-109 (for extracts cf. Ex. 256, 280, 284)—Marfa's Aria (Soprano).

" " " 16-18—Griaznov's Aria (Baritone).

Snegourotchka—The 3 songs of Lell. (Contralto).

Sadko 46-49 (cf. extract, Ex. 120)—Sadko's Aria (Tenor).

" 129-131—Lioubava's Aria (Mezzo-sopr.).

" 191-193 (cf. extract, Ex. 131)—Bass Aria.

Vocalisation.

A good vocal melody should contain notes of at least three different values, minims, crotchets and quavers (or crotchets, quavers and semiquavers etc.). Monotony in rhythmic construction is unsuited to vocal melody; it is applicable to instrumental music, but only in certain cases. *Cantabile* melody requires a fair number of long notes, and a change of syllable in a word should occur at a moment when the voice quits a long sustained note. Short, single notes, changing with every syllable produce a harmonious effect. Owing to the requirements of diction, extended melodic figures sung *legato* on one syllable must be used with care on the part of the composer; to perform these the singer must possess greater command over flexibility and technique. The possibility of taking breath in the right place is one of the conditions essential to all vocal writing. Breath cannot be taken in the middle of a word, sometimes not even during the course of a sentence or phrase in the text; hence the voice part must be suitably interspersed with rests.-135-

Table F. Voices.

Chorus:

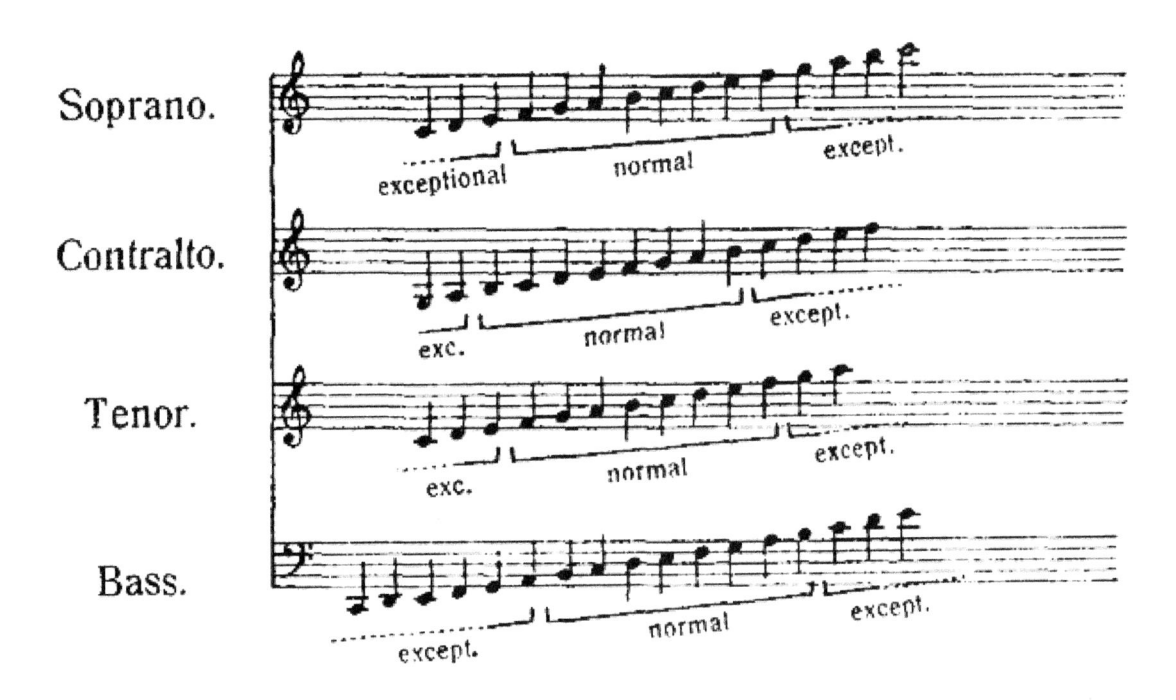

Soloists:

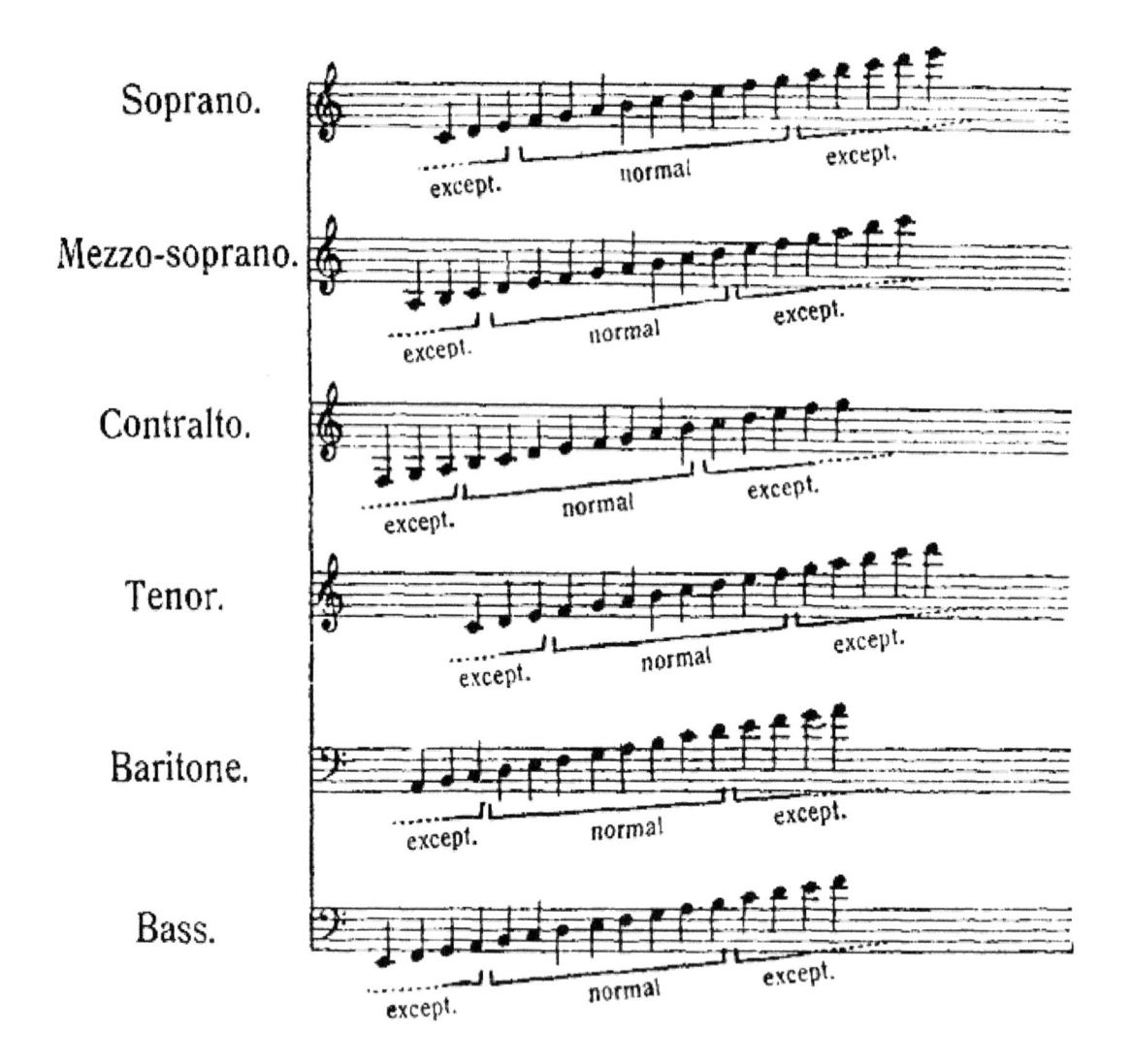

Note. It must be remembered that there are some words upon which the voice may not dwell, or sing more than one or two notes. These words may be nouns, pronouns, numerals, prepositions, conjunctions and other parts of speech. It would be impossible and ridiculous, for instance, to write a sustained note on such words as "who", "he" etc. The voice may dwell on certain words which, so to speak, possess some poetical colour.[18]

Examples:

No. 303. *Sadko* 236—Sadko's Aria (Tenor).

" 309-311 (see extract, Ex. 81). Volkhova's Cradle Song (Soprano).

Snegourotchka 9—Fairy Spring's Aria (Mezzo-sopr.).

" 187-188, 212-213 (see extracts, Ex. 102 and 225)—the two Cavatinas of Tsar Berendey (Tenor).

" 247—Miskir's Aria (Baritone).

Vowels.

As regards vocalisation on one syllable, on long sustained notes and in the high register, the choice of vowels is a matter of some importance. The difference in the position of the mouth and lips in forming the open vowel **a** and the closed vowel **ou** is apparent to everyone. The series of vowels from the point of view of open sounds is: **a**, **i**, **o**, **e**, **u**. In women's voices the easiest vowel on high notes is **a**, for men it is **o**. The vowel **i** softens the penetrating quality of the top notes of a bass voice, and the vowel **a** adds to the extension of range in the very lowest compass. Lengthy florid passages are often written on the interjection **ah**, or simply-137- on the vowel **a**. Owing to the restrictions imposed by literary and dramatic laws, the composer can only follow the above rules to a limited extent.

Examples:

Snegourotchka 293, 318-319 (cf. Ex. 119).

No. 304. *Sadko* 83.

Flexibility.

Voices possess the greatest amount of flexibility in their normal octave. Women's voices are more supple than men's, but in all types, the higher voice is the more agile, sopranos in women, the tenor voice in men. Although capable of performing florid and complicated figures, different varieties of phrasing and the rapid change from staccato to legato, the human voice is infinitely less flexible than a musical instrument. In passages of any rapidity, diatonic scales and *arpeggios* in thirds come easiest to the voice. Intervals bigger than fourths in quick succession and chromatic scales are extremely difficult. Skips of an octave or more starting from a short note should always be avoided. Preparation should precede any extremely high note either by leading up to it gradually, or by the clear leap of a fourth, fifth or octave; but sometimes the voice may attack a high note without any due preparation.

Examples:

Snegourotchka 46-48 (cf. extract, Ex. 279)—Snegourotchka's Aria (Soprano).

" 96-97—Lell's first song (Contralto).

Sadko 196-193 (cf. extract, Ex. 122)—Hindoo song (Tenor).

" 203-206—Venetian song (Baritone).

Pan Voyevoda 20-26—Maria's cradle song (Sopr).

Colour and character of voices.

The colouring of the voice, whether it be brilliant or dull, sombre or sonorous depends upon the individual singer, and the composer has no need to consider it. The chief question is interpretation and may be solved by the judicious choice of artists. From the point of view of flexibility and expression voices may be divided into two classes, *lyric* and *dramatic*. The latter is more powerful and of greater range, the former possesses more suppleness and elasticity and is more readily disposed to different shades of expression. Granted that the rare combination of the two classes is the composer's ideal, he should nevertheless be content to follow the main artistic purpose which he has set out the achieve. In complicated and important works the composer should bear in mind the characteristics of the various voices he employs; moreover, if he use two voices of the same calibre, e.g. 2 Sopranos or 2 Tenors, he should discriminate between the range and register of their respective parts, writing for one slightly higher than the other. It is no rare occurrence to meet with voices of an intermediate character (mezzo-carattere) combining the qualities of each type to a modified extent. To such voices the composer may assign rôles demanding the characteristics of each class, especially secondary rôles. At the present day, besides the rôles suitable to the dramatic and lyric type of voice, it is customary to give prominence to those demanding some special qualifications, voices of a certain tenderness or power, a specified range or degree of flexibility—attributes decided by the artistic object in view. In casting secondary and minor rôles the composer is advised to employ a medium range and less exacting demands on technique.

Note. After Meyerbeer, who was the first to write for a special type of heavy mezzo-soprano and baritone, Richard Wagner created a type of powerful dramatic soprano, of extensive range, combining the quality and scope of the soprano and mezzo-soprano voices; likewise a similar type of tenor, possessing the attributes and compass of the tenor and baritone together. To demand that voices shall be equally brilliant and resonant in the high and low register, that singers shall be endowed with a super-powerful breathing apparatus and an extraordinary faculty for resistance to fatigue (Siegfried, Parsifal, Tristan, Brünhilda, Kundry, Isolda), is to exact something little short of the miraculous. Such voices are to be found, but there are some singers with excellent though not phenomenal vocal powers, who, by the constant pursuit of Wagnerian parts endeavour to increase their range and volume, and only succeed in depriving the voice of correct intonation, beauty of tone, and all subtlety of *nuances*. I believe that less exacting demands and greater perception of what is required, skilful and judicious use of the high and low registers of the voice, a proper understanding of *cantabile* writing combined with orchestration which never overpowers the vocal part will be of greater service to the composer, from an artistic point of view, than the more elaborate methods of Richard Wagner.

Voices in combination.

Treating solo voices in a polyphonico-harmonic manner is the best method of preserving their individual character in *ensembles*. A distribution which is wholly harmonic or entirely polyphonic is seldom found. The first plan, largely used in choral writing, simplifies the movement of the voices too greatly, eliminating their melodic character; the second method is wearisome and somewhat disturbing to the ear.

As a general rule the voices are arranged according to the law of normal register. Crossing of parts is rare and should only be done with the intention of emphasising the melody in the ascending voices above those adjacent in register, e.g. the tenor part above contralto, the mezzo-soprano above the soprano, etc.

Duet.

The combinations most conducive to the proper movement of parts are those of two voices related within an octave

$$8 \begin{bmatrix} \text{Sopr., M.-sopr., C.-alto} \\ \text{Ten., Bar., Bass.} \end{bmatrix}$$

Movement in tenths, sixths, thirds or octaves (the last very seldom) will always produce satisfactory *ensemble*, and if the parts progress polyphonically, it need not happen *frequently* that they are separated by more than a tenth, or that undesirable crossing of parts will result.

Examples:

Sadko 99-101—Sopr. and Tenor (cf. Ex. 289, 290).

Servilia 143—Sopr. and Tenor.

Ivan the Terrible, Act I 48-50—Sopr. and Tenor.

Kashtcheï the Immortal 62-64. Mezzo-sopr. and Baritone.

Voices related in fifths and fourths,

$$5 \begin{bmatrix} \text{Sopr.,} \\ \text{C.-alto,} \end{bmatrix} \quad 4 \begin{bmatrix} \text{C.-alto,} \\ \text{Ten.,} \end{bmatrix} \quad 5 \begin{bmatrix} \text{Ten.} \\ \text{Bass.} \end{bmatrix}$$

should progress nearer to one another; it is rare for them to move in tenths, common in sixths and thirds; they may also proceed in unison. The two voices are seldom separated at a greater distance than an octave, and certain cases will require crossing of parts, which, however, should only be for periods of short duration.-140-

Examples:

Snegourotchka 263-264—Soprano and Alto.

* *The Christmas Night* 78-80—Alto and Tenor.

* *Legend of Kitesh* 338—Tenor and Bass.

Voices related in thirds;

3 [Sopr.,   M.-sopr., Ten., Bar.
    M.-sopr., C.-alto, Bass, Bass,

may move in unison, in thirds and sixths, and admit very largely of the crossing of parts. Separation by more than an octave must only be momentary, and is generally to be avoided.

Examples:

* *The Tsar's Bride* 174—Sopr. and Mezzo-sopr.

* *Tsar Saltan* 5-6—Sopr. and Mezzo-sopr.

In the case of voices related in twelfths:

12 [Sopr.
     Bass,

intervals approaching one another do not create a good effect, for this transplants the deeper voice into the upper register and *vice versa*. Singing in unison is no longer possible, and thirds are to be avoided; the use of sixths, tenths and thirteenths is recommended. The voices will often be separated by more than a twelfth and crossing of parts is out of the question.

Example:

* *Tsar Saltan* 254-255.

Relationship in tenths

10 [Sopr.   M.-sopr.
     Bar. or Bass

is fairly common. The explanations given above are also applicable in this case.

Example:

Snegourotchka 291-300 (cf. extract, Ex. 118) Sopr. and Bar.

The use of similar voices in pairs:

Sopr., Ten.
Sopr., Ten.

entails singing in unison and thirds. They should rarely be separated beyond a sixth, but crossing of parts is inevitable, as otherwise the resultant volume of tone would be too weak.-141-

Note. Other possible combinations:

C.-alto, M.-sopr.,
Bar., Ten.,

call for no special remarks.

Examples:

* *The May Night*, Act I pp. 59-64—Mezzo-sopr. and Tenor.

* *Sadko* 322-324—Mezzo-sopr. and Tenor.

As a general rule, writing for two voices is only successful when the progression of parts is clear, when discords are prepared by a common note, or are the outcome of conveniently separated movement and correctly resolved. Empty intervals of fourths and perfect fifths, elevenths and twelfths should be avoided on the strong beats of a bar, especially on notes of some value. If, however, one of the voices assumes a melodic character, the other forming the harmonic accompaniment in declamatory style, it is not absolutely necessary to avoid the intervals mentioned above.

Note. It is not within the scope of the present work to consider the writing of vocal parts in closer detail. This question must be left to the professor of free counterpoint. It remains to be noted that the human voice accompanied by the orchestra is always heard independently as something apart, something complete in itself. For this reason a composer may never rely on the orchestra to fill up an empty space or correct a fault in the handling of voices. All the rules of harmony and counterpoint, down to the last detail, must be applied to vocal writing, which is never dependent upon orchestral accompaniment.

Trios, quartets etc.

All that has been said regarding the relationship of voices in duet applies with equal force to the combination of three, four, five or more voices. An *ensemble* of several voices is seldom purely polyphonic; as a rule, although some parts move polyphonically, progression in thirds, sixths, tenths and thirteenths is used for the remainder. Declamation for some voices on notes forming the harmony is also possible. This variety of simultaneous movement of vocal parts renders the comprehension of the total effect less difficult for the ear, and sanctions the distribution of distinctive and suitable figures or tone colouring to certain voices with other figures or timbres which may be proceeding at the same time. The skilful arrangement of pauses and re-entries facilitates the understanding of the whole, and gives desirable prominence to detail.-142-

Examples:

Snegourotchka 267—Trio, Finale to Act III.

The Tsar's Bride 116-118—Quartet in Act II.

""" 168-171—Sextet in Act III (cf. extract, Ex. 283).

Servilia 149-152—Quintet in Act III.

The movement of solo voices is seldom purely harmonic in character with predominance given to the upper voices homophonically treated. The blending of all the parts into an harmonic whole, without any distinctive predominant feature in any one part (as in a chorale) is employed for songs or *ensembles* in traditional style, prayers, hymns, etc. If this method is adopted for the quartet of voices,

- Sopr.
- Alto
- Ten.
- Bass,

it will be noted that widely-spaced part writing is the most natural and suitable form (especially in *forte* passages), as the four voices can sing together in their proper registers (low, middle and high), while, in close part writing they may find themselves at a given moment in registers, which are entirely foreign. But both methods should be employed, as, otherwise, it would be impossible to guarantee equality in even the shortest succession of chords.

Examples:

Snegourotchka 178 Hymn of Tsar Berendey's subjects.

No. 305. *Legend of Kitesh* 341.

The second half of the last example is an instance of six-part harmonic writing; the upper voice stands out prominently, the rest form a kind of accompaniment.

Chorus.

Range and register.

The range of choral voices is slightly more limited than that of soloists. The exceptional register may be considered as two notes above and below the normal octave. The dotted lines extended still further indicate the limits upon which a composer may rely in very exceptional cases, as every full chorus must contain a few -143- voices of more than average compass, in this respect approaching the solo voice in character. In many choruses one or two bass singers may be found who are able to go still lower than the limit of the exceptional range (they are called *octavists*).[19]

Note. These uncommonly deep notes must be moderately well sustained and can only be used when the whole chorus is singing quite *piano*; they are hardly applicable except in unaccompanied choruses (*a cappella*).

The difference in range between the "firsts" and "seconds" in each type may be fixed as follows: the normal octave and the exceptionally low register should be allotted to the "seconds", the same octave and the exceptionally high register to the "firsts".

The composition of the chorus is approximately as follows: for a full chorus, 32 singers to each of the 4 parts sopr., alt., ten. and bass; for a chorus of medium size, from 16 to 20, and for a small chorus from 8 to 10 singers. The number of women will often predominate, and more voices are given to the "firsts" than to the "seconds".

On account of stage requirements a chorus may have to be divided into two or even three separate parts. This is a great disadvantage, especially with a small chorus, as each chorister becomes more or less a soloist.

The methods of writing for operatic chorus are very numerous. Besides the primary harmonico-polyphonic arrangement, containing the whole musical idea, the voices may be made to enter separately, singing or declaiming phrases of varying length; they may progress in unison or in octaves; one vocal part may repeat certain notes or the whole chorus reiterate certain chords; one melodic part may predominate (the upper part for preference), the others forming an harmonic accompaniment; isolated exclamatory phrases may be given to the whole chorus or to certain portions of it, and finally, the entire chorus may be treated in a purely harmonic manner in chords, with the essential melodic design allotted to the orchestra. Having outlined the principal methods of handling the chorus, I advise the reader to study vocal and orchestral scores where he will find many illustrations impossible to deal with here. -144-

There exists another most important operation, the division of the chorus into different groups. The most natural method is to divide it into men's chorus and women's chorus.

Less frequent combinations are altos, tenors and basses, or sopranos, altos and tenors. There remains yet another point to be considered, the sub-division of each part into two's and three's. Men's and women's choruses, considered as distinct unities may alternate either one with the other, or with the principal chorus. For this reason sub-division increases the possibilities of choral writing, and, as I have already remarked, it is only by the study of choral works that the student will acquire mastery over this branch of composition, the fundamental principles of which can only be faintly outlined in the course of the present work.

Melody.

Melody is more limited in the chorus than in the solo voice, both as regards range as well as mobility. Choristers' voices are less "settled" and not so highly trained as those of soloists. Sometimes solo and choral melody are similar in point of range and technique, but more often the latter is lacking in freedom and variety of rhythm, restricted as it is to the repetition of short phrases, while the solo voice demands broader melodic outline and greater freedom in construction. In this respect choral melody more closely resembles instrumental melody. Pauses for taking breath are not so important with chorus singers as with soloists; the former do not need to breathe all together and each singer may take a slight rest from time to time, thus obviating the necessity for sudden complete silences. The question of suitable vowels is likewise of secondary importance.

The change from notes of short value to long, vocalisation on syllables and other questions mentioned above are equally applicable to choral melody, but in a minor degree. Not more than two or three notes should be written on one syllable except for fanciful and whimsical effects.

Example:

No. 306. *The Golden Cockerel* 262; see also before 123.-145-

A. Mixed chorus.

Chorus in unison.

The simplest and most natural combination of voices is sopranos and altos, or tenors and basses. These combinations produce ample and vigourous tone, and the mixed timbres serve to give prominence to a melody in the upper or bass parts. In practice the other voices are often divided to thicken the harmony. The combination of altos and tenors produces a peculiar mixed tone quality, somewhat *bizarre* and seldom used.

Examples:

Snegourotchka 64.

Sadko 208 (cf. Ex. 14).

Progression in octaves.

The most beautiful and natural combinations are sopranos and tenors

$$8\begin{bmatrix} \text{Sopr.} \\ \text{Ten.,} \end{bmatrix}$$

altos and basses

$$8\begin{bmatrix} \text{Altos} \\ \text{Basses;} \end{bmatrix}$$

they produce a tone both brilliant and powerful. Progression of sopranos and altos, or tenors and basses is seldom practised. Though the latter combinations may occur in choruses for women and men alone, they can only be used in melodies of restricted length. The difference of register in which the voices move does not permit of the same balance of tone obtained by voices of a distinctive kind.

Examples:

Snegourotchka 60, 61—Carnival Procession.

" 113—Wedding Ceremony.

Sadko 37—Chorus of Guests, 1st Tableau.

Dividing kindred voices in octaves is seldom done,

$$8\begin{bmatrix} \text{Sopr. I} \\ \text{Sopr. II} \end{bmatrix}$$

etc., except perhaps in the basses

$$8\begin{bmatrix} \text{Basses I} \\ \text{Basses II,} \end{bmatrix}$$

when the progression of parts demand it, or it is required to double the bass part in octaves.

Examples:

Ivan the Terrible, Act III 68—Final chorus (cf. Ex. 312).

Sadko 341—Final chorus.-146-

A beautifully round tone results from doubling men's and women's voices in octaves

$$8\begin{bmatrix} \text{Sopr.} + \text{Altos} \\ \text{Ten.} + \text{Basses.} \end{bmatrix}$$

Example:

Snegourotchka 323—Final chorus.

Brilliance and vigour is achieved when sopranos and altos progress in thirds doubled in octaves by tenors and basses also in thirds:

$$8\begin{bmatrix} \text{Sopr.} \\ \text{Altos} \end{bmatrix}3 \\ \text{Ten.} \\ \text{Basses} \end{bmatrix}3.$$

Examples:

Mlada, Act I 24; Act II, before 31.

The Golden Cockerel 235.

On the rare occasions when the whole chorus progresses in double octaves the usual arrangement is:

$$\begin{matrix} \text{Sopr.} + \text{Altos} \\ 8\begin{bmatrix} \text{Ten.} \\ \text{Basses} \end{bmatrix}8, \end{matrix} \text{ or else } 8\begin{bmatrix} \text{Sopr.} \\ \text{Altos} + \text{Ten.} \\ \text{Basses} \end{bmatrix}8.$$

Examples:

Snegourotchka 319.

Sadko 182.

Voices (*divisi*); harmonic use of the mixed chorus.

The purely harmonic progression of a four-part mixed chorus is more natural and resonant when the harmony is of the widely divided order, so that the volume of tone is equally distributed throughout.

Example:

No. 307. *Sadko* 144—Beginning of 3rd tableau.

To secure a well-balanced *forte* chord in close part writing the following distribution is recommended:

[Sopr. I
[Sopr. II
  Altos
[Ten. I
[Ten. II
[Basses I
[Basses II.

-147-

Three harmonic parts in the high register (2 sopranos and altos) are doubled an octave lower by 2 tenors and the 1st basses. The lower part is undertaken by the 2nd basses. In this manner the tenors sing in the soprano octave, the 1st basses in the alto octave and the 2nd basses are independent.

Examples:

Snegourotchka 327—End of the work.

Mlada, Act II 20—Procession of Princes.

Ivan the Terrible, Act II 19 (cf. Ex. 212).

Division of parts can be adopted when one of them is entrusted with a melody, the remainder forming a sufficiently full accompaniment. The choice of parts to be divided depends upon the range of the upper one. When a harmonic-melodic phrase is repeated in different keys and registers, it may be necessary to distribute the parts and divide them in another manner, so as to maintain proper choral balance. As an illustration I give two extracts of identical musical context, the second (*F* major) being a third higher than the first (*D* major). In the first example the altos are added to the sopranos to strengthen the melody; the tenors and basses *divisi* form the harmony. In the second example the melody being a third higher may be given to the sopranos alone; the altos therefore take part in the harmony, and consequently the lower parts are divided in a different way.

Examples:

Sadko 173 and 177 (cf. Ex. 205 and 206); compare also the same music in *G* major 189.

No. 309-310. *Ivan the Terrible*, Act I 77.

Example 307 is an instance of widely-spaced four-part writing forming the harmonic basis, with the melodic idea in the orchestra. In Example 308, the same in musical context, the melodic figure is given to the sopranos, and among the other parts which form the harmony the tenors are divided.

Example:

<u>No. 308.</u> *Sadko* 152.-148-

In polyphonic writing exceeding 4 part harmony the voices should be divided so as to obtain the necessary number of actual parts. One part may be divided into as many as three different parts, 3 sopranos, 3 altos etc.

Examples:

<u>No. 312.</u> *Ivan the Terrible*, Act III 69—Final chorus.

Servilia 233—Final chorus.

Mlada, Act IV 35-36—Final chorus.

In *fugato* writing and fugal imitation for mixed chorus the distribution is generally in four parts, but this number may be increased for cumulative effects as in the example quoted. In such cases the composer should be careful as to the arrangement of the final chord, the summit and climax of the passage. After the entry of the last of the voices the progression of such a passage should be handled with a view to the tone of the final chord. The treatment should be such that concords produced by divided voices or different groups of voices retain their full value; and if the final chord be a discord its effect may be heightened by means of crossing of parts. The reader is advised to examine carefully the progression of parts leading up to the final chord in each of the examples given above, paying special attention to the distribution of these final chords. Crossing of parts must not be effected at random. The arrangement of choral parts follows the natural order of register and can only be altered for short spaces of time to give momentary prominence to some melodic or declamatory phrase.

Examples:

Ivan the Terrible, Act I 79, Act II 5, Act III 67.

B. Men's chorus and women's chorus.

In writing a three-part female chorus the division should be either

Sopr. I   Sopr.
Sopr. II or Altos I
Altos   Altos II;

the same for men:

Ten. I   Ten.
Ten. II or Bass I
Bass   Bass II.

The choice of distribution depends upon which voice is to predominate, or the register in which the group is to be placed. The manner of divid-149-ing the parts may change, one following the other at will. In four-part harmonic writing the method of division is self-evident:

Sopr. I   Ten. I
Sopr. II   Ten. II
Altos I   Bass I
Altos II Bass II

To give prominence to a melody in the middle part in three-part harmony, the following method may be adopted:

Sopr. I   Ten. I
Sopr. II + Altos I, or Ten. II + Bass I.
Altos II   Bass II

If, in three-part writing, the melody has to stand out in the upper part, the harmony may be either widely-divided or close.

Examples:

Ivan the Terrible, Act I 25-26, 23-31 (Women's chorus).

Sadko, before 181—Men's chorus (cf. Ex. 27).

No. 311. *Sadko* 270-272—Women's chorus.

In four-part choral writing close harmony is preferable, otherwise the upper part will be in too high a register and the range of the bottom part too low.

Examples:

Sadko 17—Male chorus.

Ivan the Terrible, Act II 36-38—Female chorus (cf. Ex. 296).

Distribution in two parts which is generally polyphonic does not call for any special remarks; the same may be said of chorus in unison.

Examples:

Sadko 50—Male chorus.

Mlada, beginning of Act I.

Ivan the Terrible, Act III 13-15. } Female chorus.

Servilia 26.

If male and female choruses are handled in a purely harmonic manner close part writing should be adopted. This is the only way to secure proper balance of tone in chords given to voices-150- of the same kind. Successions of chords in three parts are more frequent than those in four; sometimes a series of chords is practicable only in two parts.

Examples:

Snegourotchka 19—Chorus of Birds.

" 281-285—Chorus of Flowers (cf. Ex. 26).

In *fugato* writing, and fugal imitation in three parts, allotted to a chorus composed of voices of one kind, the principal subject is given to two parts, the counter subject to one; by this method the doubled themes will stand out to better advantage.

Examples:

Sadko 20-21.

* *The Tsar's Bride* 29-30.

Male and female choruses, apart from the part they play as individual unities, may be introduced as separate groups in mixed choruses alternating with the whole *ensemble*.

Example:

Snegourotchka 198—Hymn of Tsar Berendey's Subjects (cf. Ex. 166).

As a general rule a female chorus does not contain the real harmonic bass part when this part is situated in the low register, so that no octaves are formed between the real bass and the lower choral voice. Harmony in a chorus for women is generally given to the three upper parts, the lower part acting as accompanying bass. It will be noticed that this rule may lead to the employment of chords of the sixth and empty consecutive fourth's and fifth's which should be avoided. In example No. 311 (*Sadko* 270), this is remedied by the high position of the bass part; later an empty interval (4/5) occurs, but only for a moment, and still further on another such interval is avoided by the union of all the voices in the octave (*B/B*). In Ex. No. 304 (*Sadko* 83) the harmonic bass in the low register is carefully omitted, but when transferred to the upper register it is doubled.-151-

I conclude the present chapter with the following necessary observations:

1. The operation of dividing voices undoubtedly weakens their resonance, and as the reader will have observed, one of the principal factors in good orchestration is *equal* balance of tone in the distribution of chords. But in choral writing the question is somewhat different. The orchestra, even after repeated rehearsal always *plays from music*; the operatic chorus, on the other hand, sings by heart. The chorus master can carry out the composer's instructions as to the division of parts in one way or another, varying and adjusting the number of singers to each part. By manipulating some shade of expression he can maintain a balance of tone between divided and undivided voices. In orchestral material the composer has to handle a great number of timbres, widely different in character and volume of tone. In the chorus there are but four qualities. A chorus moving about the stage cannot convey varying shades of expression so exactly as an orchestra seated at the desk. It may therefore be safely assumed that a composer is entitled to some licence in the question of dividing choral parts; dealing with the orchestra involves greater foresight and care.

2. In trying to obtain equal balance in writing three-part choruses for male or female chorus I have often resorted to the method of doubling the middle part as recommended on p. 149. The chorus master is at liberty to equalise the chorus by transferring voices from one part to another. In choruses divided into three parts I have noticed that chorus masters are in the habit of giving the upper part to Sopr. I, or Ten. I, and the two lower parts to Sopr. II and Ten. II divided. I consider this arrangement unsound, as the balance of parts can never be equal. The attention of chorus masters is called to the necessity of strengthening middle parts, for the expedient of giving prominence to the upper part concerns melody alone and leaves harmony out of the question.

3. Skilful management of choral parts is a fairly safe guarantee of clear and satisfactory performance. Miscalculations in writing are a great hindrance to study, and the most experienced chorus may come to grief through faulty progression of parts. If the progression of parts is correct, if discords are properly prepared,-152- sudden and remote modulations, even of the harshest and most uncommon kind will be comparatively simple and may be approached with some degree of confidence. This is a fact which composers do not always bear in mind, but singers know it well and appreciate its importance to the full. As an instance I quote the very difficult modulation which occurs in Ex. No. 169 (*Sadko* 302). I doubt whether it could be sung if written in any other way. Careful endeavour on the part of a composer is better than useless struggle inflicted upon the performer.

July 31st (Aug. 13th) 1905.

FOOTNOTES

[1] This manuscript was given to me by Alexander Glazounov; if a Rimsky-Korsakov museum is ever founded it will be placed there.

[2] This preface had already been published in his *Notes and Articles on Music* (St. Petersburgh, 1911).

[3] Recently the firm of Belaieff has published Rimsky-Korsakov's symphonic works in miniature score, pocket-size.

[4] In the margin of the MS. a question mark is added here. (Editor's note.)

[5] A. Glazounov has well expressed the various degrees of excellence in scoring, which he divides into three classes: 1. When the orchestra sounds well, playing from sight; magnificent, after a few rehearsals. 2. When effects cannot be brought off except with the greatest care and attention on the part of conductor and players. 3. When the orchestra never sounds well. Evidently the chief aim in orchestration is to obtain the first of these results. (Author's note.)

[6] A short review of these various questions forms the first chapter of the book. (Editor's note.)

[7] To give a list of easy three and four-note chords, or to explain the different methods of bowing does not come within the scope of the present book.

[8] Of late years sometimes two tubas are employed, by Glazounov for instance in his Finnish Fantasia. (Editor's note.)

[A] The 7th natural harmonic is everywhere omitted as useless; the same in the horns, the notes 11, 13, 14 and 15.

[B] The $b\natural$ of the octave -1 does not exist on the trombones.

[9] A Russian instrument which, like the balalaïka, is better known abroad. (Translator's note.)

[10] A chromatic harp without pedals has now been invented in France (Lyon's system), on which the most abrupt modulations are possible. (Translator's note.)

[11] Rimsky-Korsakov's opera *Sadko* and Moussorgsky's *Boris Godounov* are particularly interesting in this respect. (Translator's note.)

[12] Recently, bells have been made of suspended metal plates possessing the rare quality of a fairly pure tone, and which are sufficiently portable to be used on the concert platform. (Editor's note.)

[C] The present volume is divided into two parts, text (pp. 1-152) and musical examples (pp. 1-333). The <u>first page of the second part</u> lists the standard full-score editions of Rimsky-Korsakov's works that are referred to throughout the book. These references to specific passages are always indicated by boxed numbers or boxed letters corresponding to the ones marking the sub-divisions of the particular score. On the other hand, references in the text to the 312 musical examples in the <u>second part</u> of the book are always indicated as "No. 1," "No. 2," etc. Thus, "*The Tsar's Bride* 84" indicates that the reader should look at section 84 of the score of *The Tsar's Bride* as published by Belaieff in Leipzig, the music of which is not reprinted here; whereas "<u>No. 1.</u> *Shéhérazade* 2nd movement B" indicates that the reader should look at the first musical example in the second part of the present book, which comes from the section marked B in the second movement of the score of *Shéhérazade* as published by Belaieff.

[13] The composer has emended the score in the following manner: from the fifth to the ninth bar after 305, and also from the fifth to the ninth bar after 306, the three clarinets play in unison, the trumpet being marked *forte* instead of *fortissimo*; in the example, the first of these passages is corrected according to the composer's alteration. (Editor's note.)

[14] The process of doubling strings and wood-wind in octaves:

$$\left.\begin{array}{l}\text{Fl.}\\ \text{Vns}\end{array}\right] 8, \quad \left.\begin{array}{l}\text{Ob.}\\ \text{'Cellos}\end{array}\right] 8,$$

etc. often used by the classics to obtain balance of tone, is not to be recommended, as the tone quality of the two groups is so widely different. As a result of the ever-increasing tendency to profusion of colour, this method has recently come into fashion again, notably among the younger French composers. (Editor's note.)

[15] In the full score a misprint occurs in the clarinet part; it is corrected in the example. (Editor's note.)

[16] A splendid example of the combination of strings and brass may be found in the introduction to the 2nd scene of the 4th act of "*Khovanstchina*" by Moussorgsky, orchestrated by Rimsky-Korsakov. (Editor's note.)

[17] Mention should be made of the happy use of a small orchestra in the wings (2 picc., 2 cl., 2 horns, 1 trombone, tambourine, 4 Vns, 2 violas, 1 D-bass) in *The May Night*, Act II, Sc. I. M-P. (Editor's note.)

[18] Here the author approaches a question so well known to the Russians that it does not require any further elucidation for their guidance. But a whole book would have to be written to form a compendium of practical rules on this subject, and to point out the

errors which nearly all French composers openly commit—even those who are famous for their sense of diction and literary style. We can only conclude that the question has come to be considered of minor importance in France, perhaps on account of the lack of definite stress on the syllables of words, which is characteristic of the French language. It is not within the translator's province to discuss the question of French versification or to elaborate the excellent maxims laid down by Rimsky-Korsakov, the first, among many, to touch upon this delicate and important subject. (Translator's note.)

[19] *Contrebasses* voices as they are called when mentioned in French works are peculiar to Russia, in which country they are plentiful. (Translator's note.)

Printed in Great Britain
by Amazon